Boston Tea Parties

Recipes from the Museum of Fine Arts, Boston

Compiled and Edited by:

JUDITH F. CHAMBERLAIN *and* JANET R. SEARS

THANK YOU:
We wish to thank the members of the Ladies Committee, Ladies Committee Associates, staff, and friends for generously sharing their valued recipes. Many were contributed anonymously and many were duplicates, making it impossible to credit donors for their recipes. However, to all who helped we are most grateful.

ISBN 0-87846-281-3

Library of Congress catalogue card
no. 87-61474

Type set by Schooley Graphics, Dayton, Ohio

Printed by Acme Printing Company
Wilmington, Massachusetts

Designed by Carl Zahn

Cover and title-page illustration:
MARY CASSATT (American, 1844-1926)
Five O'Clock Tea; oil painting, 1880
M. Theresa B. Hopkins Fund

Contents

AMERICAN, 1750–1775
Tea table; mahogany with 18th-century garniture
The M. and M. Karolik Collection of 18th-century American Arts

Foreword

The serving of afternoon tea by members of the Ladies Committee is one of the activities of these volunteers most appreciated by our visitors. Especially those who come from afar have come to regard this as a typical Bostonian tradition, not realizing that it is—by Boston standards—a relatively new one. It was initiated shortly after the founding of the Ladies Committee in 1956 and goes back, therefore, about twenty-five years.

With the reopening of the Evans Wing, the Ladies Committee contributed the funds to convert the former Fenway foyer into an attractive new and now permanent site to continue the gracious custom of serving tea and providing, at the same time, musical entertainment, often offered by young musicians.

After the great successes of the Museum's two cookbooks, which first appeared in 1970 and 1981, respectively, and which have been reprinted many times, it is fitting that the third cookbook in this series should address itself to tea and its many accompaniments. We hope that this book will generate a new interest in tea and all that comes with it, as well as the thrill of discovery of the many works of art in the Museum's great collections.

JAN FONTEIN
Director

Teatime

With the renovated Evans Wing emerges the Ladies Committee Gallery, space for the custom of afternoon tea to continue. In a charming atmosphere of chamber music, a pleasant afternoon tea is served from a table set with gleaming silver tea accessories, properly brewed tea, and a tray full of fresh-baked delights. A perfect way to relax and enjoy your Museum experience.

Tea

A steaming cup of tea quenches the thirst and soothes the spirit. One of life's greatest pleasures is the rich taste of tea that is freshly brewed. The care with which tea is prepared is as important as the variety of tea selected.

How to brew the perfect pot:

1. Rinse with hot water to condition a china or earthenware teapot.
2. Put 1 teaspoon of tea in the pot for each cup desired, plus one for the pot.
3. Bring fresh, cold water to a full rolling boil, pour over the tea, and allow to steep covered for 3-5 minutes. (Overbrewing causes a bitter taste in tea.) Remove holder or tea ball.
4. Use a "tea cozy" to keep the tea hot while steeping and serving.

Serve tea accompanied with sweets, breads, or sandwiches. Whether the tea menu is simple or elaborate, it should be interesting and distinctive.

Basic Techniques

Plan before starting to bake; read the recipe and directions completely. Assemble all equipment and ingredients necessary. Methods of mixing and order of combining ingredients are important in many products. For example, a basic principle for cookies of all kinds: never work or beat dough after flour has been added; it will make the cookies tough. Additional tips will be discussed at the beginning of each unit.

Preheat

Set oven at temperature specified by the recipe and preheat for 15 minutes before baking. Do not open oven while baking, except toward the end of the time specified to test.

Melt

To liquefy an ingredient by low heat.

Scald

In a saucepan heat milk to a temperature just below boiling point. A thin skin forming over surface and a row of tiny bubbles appearing around edge indicates sufficient heating.

Cream

Work food until soft and fluffy. Beat softened butter with an electric mixer or rub against side of bowl with the back of a wooden spoon until smooth and fluffy. Gradually add sugar and continue mixing until light.

Beat

With an electric mixer at high speed, briskly blend ingredients over and over to enclose air and make the mixture light. By hand use a vertical circular motion.

Stir

Mix at medium-low speed with an electric mixer only until all ingredients are blended. By hand hold spoon upright and use a horizontal circular motion.

Blend or Mix

Combine two or more ingredients so that each loses its identity.

Whip

Rapidly beat light mixtures such as egg whites and creams.

Fold

Combine two prepared mixtures, the lighter one on top of the heavier. Use rubber spatula to cut down gently through center of mixtures, lift and fold over ingredients lightly. Repeat carefully until blended.

Knead

If using an electric mixer equipped with a dough hook, knead at medium-low speed 2 or 3 minutes. If kneading by hand use a push-turn-fold motion. Use lower part of hand (heel) to push, turn dough ¼ way around after each push, fold over and repeat motions for 8-10 minutes, until dough is smooth and elastic. Occasionally break rhythm by slamming dough against work surface.

Utensils and Equipment

All measurements are level unless otherwise stated in recipe. Even a small variation in the amount of an ingredient can change the balance of the recipe enough to cause poor results. Use standard measuring cups and spoons that conform to United States Bureau of Standards specification.

Liquid Measure

Use glass cup with measurements marked on the side and with a top that extends above cup line to prevent spilling. For accuracy, set measuring cup on a level surface, fill by pouring liquid into cup, and check exact amount at eye level.

Dry Ingredients

Use metal nested cups available in sets of four (¼ cup, ⅓ cup, ½ cup, and 1 cup). These do not have extensions above the cup measure nor do they have lips. For a level measurement sift or lightly spoon dry ingredient into cup, then draw a straight metal spatula across the top. However, *brown sugar* needs to be *packed* into the cup so firmly that it holds the shape of the cup when turned out. An easy way to measure *butter* is by *weight.* Allow ½ pound for 1 cup, ¼ pound for ½ cup; other amounts are determined by print marks on butter. Otherwise, press shortening into a dry measuring cup, packing it tightly, and level off at top. If desired, any solid vegetable shortening may be substituted for butter, with one exception: 1 cup of butter equals ⅞ cup of lard.

Measuring Spoons

The standard set includes 1 tablespoon, 1 teaspoon, ½ teaspoon, and ¼ teaspoon. Fill spoon heaping full and level off with a straight metal spatula.

JAPANESE, 19th century
Four tea bags; brocade silk
Gift of Denman Waldo Ross

Ingredients

Flour Sifter

A sifter or sieve is needed to sift some ingredients before measuring and to help combine dry ingredients together before adding to batter. Flour has a tendency to pack on standing, so always sift flour once before measuring, even if the flour label says pre-sifted.

Rubber Spatula

A spatula is useful for scraping the bowl while adding ingredients, so the batter is well combined. It is handy for scraping the batter from the bowl and is helpful for folding ingredients.

Baking Sheets and Pans

Use size and type of pan specified in recipe for best results. The wrong size means uneven baking and products with poor texture and appearance. A wide selection of heavy-gauge stainless-steel or aluminum equipment is readily available. Aluminum-clad baking equipment lined with stainless steel reflects the heat away from product and produces even browning. If a glass pan is used, set oven temperature 25° lower than temperature mentioned in recipe. Each recipe specifies whether pans are greased, lined and greased, or ungreased. For greasing use oil or very soft vegetable shortening and rub well until a thin film of grease covers the bottom and corners.

Cooling Racks

Remove baked products to wire racks for cooling so that the air can circulate around them.

Success starts with the freshest and finest ingredients, those of high, uniform quality. Each ingredient has a special function in baking and contributes its own quality to the finished product. Use only ingredients mentioned in recipe; do not improvise, as substitutes can never guarantee the same results. All ingredients should be at *room temperature* before combining together. Ingredients in this book are defined in the following form in the recipes.

Butter

Salted butter keeps longer than sweet butter. Store in the refrigerator up to 3 weeks and in the freezer for 6 months. Sweet (or unsalted) butter is richer in flavor because of the higher ratio of cream to water. Store in refrigerator up to 1 week or in the freezer 2 months.

Sugar

Use white, fine granulated sugar. Brown sugar refers to light brown sugar, unless stated as dark brown sugar. Confectioners' sugar is 10-X powdered sugar, which should be sifted before measuring and using.

Eggs

Use *large* grade A eggs, unless otherwise stated. To test for freshness, place egg in deep container of cold water. A fresh egg sinks to the bottom; a stale egg floats.

Flour

Use white, all-purpose flour, which is a blend of hard and soft wheat flours. It may be either bleached or unbleached. Cake flour is a highly refined flour, milled from soft wheat, which must be sifted before measuring. Whole-wheat flour is a flour milled from cleaned whole-wheat grain. Do not sift; just stir flour and lightly spoon it into measuring cup.

Baking Powder

Use fresh double-action baking powder.

Soda

Use pure baking soda (sodium bicarbonate).

Cocoa

Use unsweetened cocoa powder. Do not substitute prepared cocoa mix.

Chocolate Chips

Use semi-sweet chocolate chips, unless stated as milk-chocolate chips.

Oatmeal

Quick oatmeal is 1-minute rolled oats (use uncooked). Old-fashioned oatmeal is 5-minute rolled oats (use uncooked).

Spices

Measurements are for *ground* spices unless otherwise described. Store in airtight container to seal in flavor.

Peel

Grate lightly to get only the colored portion of peel for the zest. Do not grate deeply because pith (white part) underneath tends to be bitter.

Fruits

Dried fruits (dates, raisins, currants) must be soft and fresh because baking will not soften them. If they have become too dry, plump by steaming over hot water for a few minutes and dry between layers of paper towels. *Do not* substitute prepared chopped, sugared dates in recipe.

Nuts

Use freshly shelled nuts. Unless a specified nut is suggested in a recipe, pecans, walnuts, and almonds can be substituted.

Yeast

Yeast is sold in dry and moist forms. One package of granular yeast can be substituted for one cake of moist yeast.

GREEK, ca. 340 B.C.
Votive relief to Helios and Mên; marble
Frederick Brown Fund

Equivalent Weights and Measures

	pinch, dash		= less than ⅛ teaspoon
	60 drops		= 1 teaspoon
	3 teaspoons		= 1 tablespoon
	2 tablespoons		= 1 liquid ounce
	4 tablespoons		= ¼ cup
	5 tablespoons + 1 teaspoon		= ⅓ cup
	16 tablespoons		= 1 cup
	1 cup		= 8 liquid ounces
	16 ounces		= 1 pound
Sugar:	granulated	1 pound	= 2 cups
	brown	1 pound	= 2¼ cups, firmly packed
	confectioners'	1 pound	= 4 cups
Flour:	all-purpose	1 pound	= 4 cups, sifted
	cake	1 pound	= 4½ cups, sifted
	whole wheat	1 pound	= 3½ cups, stirred
Eggs: (large)	egg whites	8-10	= 1 cup
	egg yolks	10-14	= 1 cup
	whole eggs	4-6	= 1 cup
Butter:	1 pound		= 2 cups
	1 cup		= 16 tablespoons
Nuts:	almonds	1 pound	= 3½ cups, shelled
	peanuts	1 pound	= 3 cups, shelled
	pecans	1 pound	= 4 cups, shelled
	walnuts	1 pound	= 4 cups, shelled
Dried fruits:	candied fruits	1 pound	= 3 cups, cut up
	candied peels	1 pound	= 3 cups, cut up
	dates	1 pound	= 2 cups, pitted
	prunes	1 pound	= 2½ cups, pitted
	raisins, seedless	1 pound	= 3¼ cups

Note: Whole, pitted, cut-up, and finely chopped ingredients measure differently.

Bar Cookies

Bar cookies are made from stiff dough that is spread or pressed into a shallow pan. They are cut into bars or different shapes after baking, when slightly cooled. Cut with a very sharp knife or a large pizza cutter.

Care should be taken not to overmix the dough. Stir dry ingredients only until moistened; otherwise, cookies will develop a tough texture and crusty tops. Use pan size recommended. If too large, cookies will be dry; if too small, cookies may not bake through. Spread dough evenly in pan so it will bake uniformly.

Bake until the top springs back when touched gently with your finger, or until cake tester inserted in center comes out clean. Bar cookies should have a texture that is fine, tender, and slightly moist.

Brownie Crisps

½ cup butter
1 oz. unsweetened chocolate
1 tsp. instant coffee
½ cup sugar
1 egg
¼ tsp. vanilla
¼ tsp. salt
¼ cup flour
½ cup finely chopped nuts

Melt butter and chocolate over low heat in a heavy saucepan. Stir until smooth. Add instant coffee and stir to dissolve. Remove from heat and stir in sugar, then egg and vanilla. Mix thoroughly. Add salt and flour; mix until smooth. Pour into a greased 15x10-inch jelly-roll pan and spread evenly. Sprinkle with nuts. Bake in a 375° oven on center rack exactly 15 minutes, reversing position of pan once during baking to insure even browning. Remove from oven and without waiting, cut carefully with a sharp knife. Immediately, before cookies cool and harden, remove them with a wide spatula. Cool on rack. Store in air-tight container.

Yield: 5 dozen

Thin Chocolate Squares

½ cup butter, softened
1 cup brown sugar, packed
2 eggs, beaten
2 oz. unsweetened chocolate, melted
½ cup flour
1 tsp. vanilla
1 cup chopped nuts
confectioners' sugar

Cream butter and sugar. Add beaten eggs, chocolate, flour, vanilla and nuts. Spread the batter evenly on a greased and floured 10x15-inch baking sheet. Bake in a 325° oven for 10-12 minutes. Sprinkle the top with confectioners' sugar while still warm and cut into squares.

Thin Chocolate Cookies

½ cup butter
2 oz. unsweetened chocolate
1 cup sugar
2 eggs
¾ cup flour
½ tsp. vanilla

Melt butter with chocolate, add sugar; cream well. Add eggs, one at a time, mix well before adding flour and vanilla. Spread very thin on a greased 15x10-inch jelly-roll pan. Bake in a 350° oven for 8-10 minutes. Baking is completed when cookie springs back when touched with finger. Cut immediately and remove from pan. (If cookie sticks, return briefly to oven).

Yield: 5 dozen

SCOTT PRIOR (American, b. 1949)
Nanny and Rose; oil painting, 1983
Gift of the Stephen and Sybil Stone Foundation

Jon Vie Brownies

2 cups sugar
1 cup brown sugar, packed
⅔ cup light corn syrup
1 cup butter, softened
6 eggs
6 oz. unsweetened chocolate
2 cups flour
2 cups pecans, chopped

Beat together the sugars, corn syrup and butter. Mix in eggs, one at a time, just until absorbed. Melt chocolate and add to mixture. Add flour, stir until blended. Reserve ½ cup of nuts and stir in the rest. Pour into an *ungreased* 15x10x2-inch pan, sprinkle remaining ½ cup of pecans on top and bake for 40 minutes in a 350° oven, or until a cake tester inserted in center comes out clean. Cool; cut into bars.

Yield: 5 dozen

Fudgies

16 oz. semi-sweet chocolate, finely chopped
1 cup sweet butter, cut in pieces
⅓ cup strong coffee
4 eggs
1½ cups sugar
½ cup flour
2 cups walnuts, coarsely chopped

In the top of a double boiler set over hot water, melt the chocolate, butter and coffee, stirring frequently until smooth. Remove the pan from heat and cool, stirring occasionally for 10 minutes. Beat eggs until frothy. Gradually add the sugar and continue to beat for 2 minutes, or until the mixture is very light and fluffy. Reduce speed to low and gradually beat in the chocolate mixture until just blended. Stir in flour and walnuts. Do not overbeat the mixture. Transfer the batter to a 13x9x2-inch baking pan lined with a double thickness of aluminum foil so that the foil extends 2 inches beyond the sides of the pan. Grease the bottom and sides of the foil-lined pan. Bake in a 375° oven for 25-30 minutes or until just set around the edges and moist in the center. Cool in the pan on a rack for 30 minutes. Cover the pan tightly with aluminum foil and refrigerate overnight. Remove the top foil and run a sharp knife around the edge. Using two ends of the foil as handles, lift onto a large plate and peel off the foil. Invert them again onto a smooth surface and cut into rectangles.

Yield: 4 dozen

Fudge Brownies

1 Tblsp. cocoa
½ cup sweet butter, melted
8 oz. semi-sweet chocolate, coarsely chopped
2 eggs
2 tsp. vanilla
¾ cup sugar
⅓ cup sour cream
¼ cup flour
¼ tsp. baking powder
¼ tsp. salt
½ cup chopped walnuts

Generously grease an 8x8x2-inch pan and dust with cocoa, tapping out excess. Pour hot melted butter over chocolate and let stand for 5 minutes; stir well. Beat eggs with vanilla until frothy. Add sugar gradually, and continue beating until light and thick. Stir warm chocolate into egg mixture. Stir in sour cream. Sift together flour, baking powder and salt; stir into chocolate mixture, alternating with walnuts, until blended. Pour batter into prepared pan and bake for 50-55 minutes in a 325° oven, until a cake tester comes out clean. Cool and cut.

Yield: 2½ dozen

Best-Ever Dessert Brownies

2 oz. unsweetened chocolate
½ cup butter
2 eggs
1 cup sugar
1 tsp. vanilla
½ cup flour
⅛ tsp. salt
¾ cup chopped nuts
6 oz. chocolate chips
½ cup sour cream

Melt chocolate and butter in a small pan over low heat; cool. Beat eggs well, gradually beat in sugar until mixture is thick. Stir in chocolate mixture and vanilla. Fold in flour and salt until well blended, stir in nuts. Spread evenly in an 8x8x2-inch greased pan. Bake in a 350° oven for 30 minutes. Cool completely in pan. Melt chocolate chips in top of double boiler, stir until smooth, remove from heat, stir in sour cream until blended. Spread frosting over brownies.

Yield: 2½ dozen

Basic Brownies

⅔ cup flour
¼ tsp. salt
½ tsp. baking powder
⅓ cup butter
2 oz. unsweetened chocolate
2 eggs
1 cup sugar
1 tsp. vanilla
½ cup chopped walnuts

Sift flour with salt and baking powder. Melt butter and chocolate over hot water. Beat eggs well, add sugar gradually, beating well after each addition. Beat in chocolate; stir in dry ingredients, vanilla and nuts. Bake in a greased 8x8x2-inch pan in 350° oven about 25 minutes. Cool in pan.

Variations: Peanut Butter Brownies
Omit the chopped walnuts and place miniature Reese's Peanut Butter Cups into the batter, in the pan, arrange so that each square will have a cup.

Rich Basic Brownies
Follow above recipe, but use 2 cups sugar, 4 oz. unsweetened chocolate and 1 cup chopped nuts. Important to beat eggs and sugar until sugar dissolves. Bake in a greased 11x7x2-inch pan for 45-50 minutes in a 350° oven.

Yield: 2½ dozen

Favorite Brownies

½ cup butter
2 oz. unsweetened chocolate
½ cup sugar
¾ cup dark brown sugar, packed
2 eggs
½ cup flour
¼ tsp. salt
½ tsp. soda
1 tsp. vanilla
½ cup chopped nuts

Melt butter and chocolate over low heat, stirring occasionally. Add sugars and stir until dissolved. Remove pan from heat and allow to cool. When cool, beat in eggs, one at a time, beating until mixture is shiny. Stir in flour, salt and soda, which has been sifted together. Add vanilla and nuts; mix well. Pour batter into an 8x8x2-inch greased pan and bake in a 350° oven for 30 minutes or until a tester comes out clean. Do not overcook. Cool in pan. Cut in squares and remove from pan.

Yield: 2½ dozen

DUTCH OR ENGLISH, mid-18th century
Fan; painted
The Elizabeth Day McCormick Collection

Marshmallow Brownies

2 oz. unsweetened chocolate
½ cup butter
1 cup sugar
2 eggs
1 tsp. vanilla
½ cup flour
¾ cup chopped nuts
¾ cup miniature marshmallows

Melt chocolate, cool. Cream together butter and sugar, add eggs one at a time, beating well after each addition. Add vanilla, cooled chocolate, flour and nuts. Pour into an 8x8x2-inch greased pan and bake in a 325° oven for 32 minutes. Remove from oven and cover with marshmallows, return to oven for 1½ minutes, remove and gently press melted marshmallows together. Pour chocolate frosting over marshmallows. Cool for an hour and refrigerate.

Frosting:
¼ cup hot water
1 oz. unsweetened chocolate
2 Tblsp. butter
2 cups confectioners' sugar
1 tsp. vanilla

Melt water, chocolate and butter over low heat. Remove from heat and mix in sugar and vanilla. Pour over marshmallows on brownies.

Yield: 2½ dozen

Chewy Brownies

⅓ cup butter
2 oz. unsweetened chocolate
1 cup sugar
2 eggs
⅓ tsp. salt
½ cup flour
½ cup chopped nuts
1 tsp. vanilla

Melt butter and chocolate in top of double boiler. Remove from heat and add remaining ingredients. Pour into well-greased 8x8x2-inch pan and bake in 325° oven for 25 minutes.

Yield: 2½ dozen

Marble Brownies

1 cup butter, softened
2¼ cups brown sugar, packed
1 tsp. vanilla
dash salt
2 eggs, extra-large
2⅓ cups flour
½ cup shredded coconut
¼ cup butter
1 can sweetened condensed milk
12 oz. chocolate chips

Cream 1 cup butter, sugar, vanilla and salt. Add eggs, one at a time, beating well after each addition. Beat until creamy. Blend in flour and coconut, just until mixed. Combine ¼ cup butter, milk and chocolate chips in a double boiler. Whip with wire whisk until smooth. Spread ⅔ of the vanilla batter in greased 13x9x2-inch baking pan. Cover with chocolate mixture. Dot remaining ⅓ vanilla batter over top, leaving exposed chocolate spots. Bake in a 350° oven for 40-45 minutes, or until golden brown. Time is critical, better to underbake than overbake. Cut when cool.

Yield: 4 dozen

Chocolate Half-Way Cookies

½ cup butter
1 cup sugar
2 eggs, separated
2 Tblsp. water
1 tsp. vanilla
2 cups flour
½ tsp. salt
¼ tsp. soda
1 tsp. baking powder
6 oz. chocolate chips
1 cup brown sugar, packed
½ cup chopped walnuts

Cream butter and sugar. Add egg yolks, slightly beaten with 2 Tblsp. water. Add vanilla. Sift together flour, salt, soda and baking powder; stir into creamed mixture. Press dough into greased 15x10-inch jelly-roll pan. Press chocolate chips into dough. Beat egg whites until stiff; fold in brown sugar and walnuts. Spread on top of dough. Bake in a 325° oven for 20-25 minutes.

Yield: 5 dozen

Black-Bottom Brownies

1½ cups flour
1 cup sugar
¼ cup cocoa
1 tsp. soda
1 cup water
⅓ cup oil
1 Tblsp. vinegar
1 tsp. vanilla

Sift dry ingredients into mixing bowl. Add remaining ingredients. Mix well. Pour into 13x9x2-inch greased pan, cover with topping.

Topping:
8 oz. cream cheese
1 egg
⅓ cup sugar
⅛ tsp. salt
6 oz. chocolate chips
½ cup sugar
½ cup chopped walnuts

Combine softened cream cheese with egg, add 1/3 cup sugar and salt, beating well. Fold in chocolate chips. Spoon over batter in pan. Combine ½ cup sugar and nuts, sprinkle on top. Bake 40 minutes in a 350° oven.

Yield: 4 dozen

Chocolate-Orange Bars

1¼ cups flour
¾ tsp. soda
½ tsp. salt
¾ cup brown sugar
½ cup water
½ cup butter
1¼ cups chopped dates
6 oz. chocolate chips, melted
2 eggs, beaten
½ cup orange juice
½ cup milk
1 cup chopped walnuts

Sift together flour, soda and salt; set aside. Heat sugar, water, butter and dates until dates soften. Cool. Add chocolate and eggs. Stir well. Add dry ingredients alternately with juice and milk. Stir in nuts. Bake in a greased 15x10x2-inch pan for 25-30 minutes in a 350° oven.

Orange Glaze Frosting:
1½ cups confectioners' sugar
2 Tblsp. butter, softened
2-3 Tblsp. cream
1 Tblsp. grated orange peel
½ tsp. orange extract

Blend until smooth. Frost bars when cool.

Yield: 5 dozen

Iced Orange-Hazelnut Brownies

1/2 cup butter
2 oz. unsweetened chocolate, broken in pieces
2 eggs
3/4 cup sugar
1 tsp. vanilla
2 tsp. grated orange peel
1/2 cup flour
1/2 tsp. baking powder
pinch salt
1/2 cup hazelnuts, toasted, peeled and coarsely chopped

Melt butter and chocolate together. Cool about 5 minutes. Beat eggs, sugar, vanilla and orange peel thoroughly; beat in cooled chocolate mixture. Sift together flour, baking powder and salt, add to chocolate mixture. Add chopped nuts. Pour batter into a well-greased 9x9x2-inch pan and bake in a 350° oven for 20-25 minutes. Remove from oven and cool on rack. Frost when cool.

Grand Marnier Frosting:
1/2 cup heavy cream
6 oz. semi-sweet chocolate, broken in pieces
2 Tblsp. sweet butter, softened
1/2 tsp. vanilla
1 Tblsp. Grand Marnier

Heat cream in heavy saucepan, remove from heat and add chocolate pieces. Return to low heat and stir until chocolate is melted. Add butter, vanilla, Grand Marnier. Stir until mixture is smooth and shiny. Cool until thick enough to spread. Refrigerate. Cut into squares when frosting is firm.

Yield: 3 dozen

Chocolate Revel Bars

1 cup butter, softened
2 cups brown sugar, packed
2 eggs
2 tsp. vanilla
3 cups quick oatmeal
2 1/2 cups flour
1 tsp. soda
1 1/2 tsp. salt
1 can sweetened condensed milk
12 oz. chocolate chips
2 Tblsp. butter
1 cup chopped walnuts
2 tsp. vanilla

Cream butter and brown sugar until light and fluffy. Beat in eggs and 2 tsp. vanilla. Mix together oatmeal, flour, soda and 1 tsp. salt and add to creamed mixture, blend well. Set aside. In heavy saucepan stir milk, chocolate, 2 Tblsp. butter and 1/2 tsp. salt over low heat until smooth. Remove from heat. Stir in nuts and 2 tsp. vanilla. Pat 2/3 of oatmeal mixture into *ungreased* 15x10-inch jelly-roll pan. Spread chocolate mixture over oatmeal layer, sprinkle with remaining oatmeal mixture. Bake for 25-30 minutes in a 350° oven. Cool. Cut into bars.

Yield: 5 dozen

Armenian Fudge Bars

Filling:
12 oz. chocolate chips
8 oz. cream cheese
⅔ cup sweetened condensed milk
1 cup walnuts
½ tsp. almond extract *or* vanilla

Combine chocolate chips, cream cheese and milk in double boiler, melt over hot water. Beat until well blended, add nuts and flavoring. Set aside.

Crust:
3 cups flour
1½ cups sugar
1 tsp. baking powder
½ tsp. salt
1 cup butter, softened
2 eggs
½ tsp. almond extract *or* vanilla

Combine dry ingredients, cut in butter and add remaining ingredients until mixture resembles coarse crumbs. Press ½ mixture in greased 15x10x2-inch pan. Spread chocolate filling over crumbs. Sprinkle remaining crumbs on top. Bake 30-35 minutes or until lightly browned in a 375° oven.

Yield: 5 dozen

Chocolate Peppermint Squares

2 oz. unsweetened chocolate
½ cup butter
2 eggs, beaten
1 cup sugar
¼ tsp. peppermint extract
dash salt
½ cup flour
½ cup chopped walnuts

Melt chocolate and butter over hot water; set aside. Cream together eggs, sugar, peppermint extract and salt. Add chocolate mixture. Stir in flour and nuts. Pour into greased 9x9x2-inch pan and bake in a 350° oven for 20-25 minutes. Cool and spread frosting.

Peppermint Frosting:
2 Tblsp. butter, softened
1 cup confectioners' sugar
1 Tblsp. cream
¾ tsp. peppermint extract

Mix above ingredients together until smooth. Frost cake and refrigerate until chilled and set.

Glaze:
1 oz. unsweetened chocolate
1 Tblsp. butter

Melt together chocolate and butter. Drizzle over cake, tilting pan until glaze covers all. Refrigerate 5 minutes to firm glaze. Cut into squares.

Yield: 3 dozen

Raspberry Brownies

⅓ cup butter
2 oz. unsweetened chocolate
2 eggs
1 cup sugar
1 tsp. raspberry liqueur
⅔ cup flour
¼ tsp. salt
½ tsp. baking powder
½ cup broken walnuts
raspberry jam

Melt butter and chocolate over hot water; set aside. Beat eggs well and gradually add sugar. Beat chocolate mixture into eggs. Add raspberry liqueur. Stir in sifted dry ingredients; add nuts. Pour in a greased 8x8x2-inch pan. Drop small quantities of raspberry jam in the center of each square. Bake in a 350° oven for 25 minutes. Cool in pan before cutting.

Yield: 2½ dozen

Vienna Raspberry-Chocolate Bars

1 cup butter
2 egg yolks
1½ cups sugar
2½ cups flour
10-oz. jar raspberry jelly
1 cup chocolate chips
4 egg whites
¼ tsp. salt
2 cups finely chopped nuts

Cream butter with egg yolks and ½ cup sugar. Add flour and knead. Pat batter on a greased 15x10-inch jelly-roll pan. Bake in a 350° oven for 15-20 minutes until lightly browned. Remove from oven, spread with jelly and top with chocolate chips. Whip egg whites with salt until stiff, gradually beat in remaining sugar (1 cup). Fold in nuts. Gently spread on top of jelly and chocolate. Bake about 25 minutes in 350° oven. Cut into squares.

Yield: 5 dozen

Jolly Jam Bars

1 cup butter
1 cup sugar
2 egg yolks
2 cups flour
1 cup chopped walnuts or pecans
green food coloring (optional)
½ cup raspberry jam

Cream butter and sugar until light and fluffy. Add egg yolks and continue beating. Gradually add flour, mix. Add nuts and blend well. Divide dough in half and, if desired tint one part. Press first layer of dough evenly into greased 9x9x2-inch pan. Top with jam; cover with remaining dough. Bake in a 325° oven for 45-60 minutes. Cool and cut into bars.

Yield: 3 dozen

Raspberry Bars

Crumb mixture:
2¼ cups flour
1 cup chopped pecans
1 cup sugar
1 cup butter, softened
1 egg

Filling:
10-oz. jar raspberry preserves

Mix all ingredients, except raspberry preserves. Beat at low speed, scraping sides of bowl often, until mixture is crumbly (2-3 minutes). Reserve 1½ cups crumb mixture; set aside. Press remaining crumb mixture into greased 8x8x2-inch pan. Spread preserves to within ½ inch from edge of unbaked crumb mixture. Crumble remaining crumb mixture over preserves. Bake in 350° oven for 42-50 minutes, or until lightly browned. Cool and cut into bars.

Yield: 2½ dozen

Jam Squares

½ cup butter
1 cup sugar
2 eggs, separated
1 cup flour
10-oz. jar seedless raspberry jam
1⅓ cups shredded coconut

Cream butter and ½ cup sugar, add egg yolks, and flour, mixing well. Pat into *ungreased* 13x9x2-inch pan. Spread with jam. Bake 15 minutes in a 350° oven. Beat 2 egg whites until stiff, gradually beating in ½ cup sugar. Fold in shredded coconut. Spread over baked cookies, return to oven and bake an additional 25 minutes. When cool, cut into squares.

Yield: 4 dozen

Raspberry Yum-Yums

1 cup butter
½ cup confectioners' sugar
1 egg yolk
½ tsp. vanilla
2½ cups sifted cake flour
½ tsp. salt
1 egg white + pinch salt
¼ cup sugar
1 tsp. cinnamon
1¼ cups chopped nuts
seedless raspberry jam

Cream butter, add sugar gradually, beat until mixture is light and fluffy. Add egg yolk and vanilla. Beat until light. Sift flour and salt, add to batter gradually. Turn into greased 9x9x2-inch pan. Smooth batter down by pressing with another pan the same size (grease the bottom). Chill for at least 1 hour or overnight. Cover batter with jam. Beat egg white until frothy, sprinkle with salt, add ¼ cup of sugar 2 Tblsp. at a time, beating constantly. Add cinnamon and beat until stiff. Spread egg white over jam and sprinkle with chopped nuts. Bake 25-30 minutes in a 350° oven. Cool in pan before cutting.

Yield: 3 dozen

Linzer Bars

½ cup butter, softened
½ cup brown sugar, packed
¼ cup sugar
⅔ cup almonds, ground and toasted
1 egg, beaten
1½ cups flour
¾ tsp. baking powder
½ tsp. cinnamon
¼ tsp. salt
¾ cup raspberry jam
1 tsp. grated lemon peel
confectioners' sugar

Cream butter and sugars until the mixture is light and fluffy; stir in almonds and egg. Sift together flour, baking powder, cinnamon and salt, stir the mixture into the creamed mixture, and combine the dough well. Press two thirds of the dough into a greased 8x8x2-inch pan, spread with raspberry jam that has been combined with lemon peel. Roll out remaining dough ⅛ inch thick between sheets of waxed paper and chill for 15 minutes. Peel off the top sheet, cut into ½ inch strips and arrange in a lattice pattern on top of jam. Bake in a 375° for 30 minutes. Sift confectioners' sugar evenly over top. Cut into squares when cool.

Yield: 3 dozen

Nutmeg Cake Squares

1½ cups brown sugar, packed
2 cups flour
½ cup butter, cut in pieces
1 egg, beaten
1 tsp. freshly grated nutmeg
1 cup buttermilk
1 tsp. soda
¾ cup coarsely chopped cashews

Blend sugar and flour, add butter and cut into dry ingredients to make small crumbs, use either pastry blender or food processor. Press half the crumbs into a greased 9x9x2-inch pan. To remaining crumbs, add egg, nutmeg and buttermilk, which has been mixed with soda. Pour batter over crumb mixture in baking pan and sprinkle with chopped nuts. Bake in a 350° oven for 35 minutes. Cut when cool.

Yield: 3 dozen

Rocky-Road Bars

½ cup butter
1 cup sugar
1 egg, whole
2 eggs, separated
1½ cups flour
1 tsp. baking powder
¼ tsp. salt
1 cup nuts, chopped
½ cup chocolate chips
1 cup miniature marshmallows
1 cup brown sugar, packed

Cream butter and sugar. Beat in whole egg and 2 egg yolks. Sift flour, baking powder and salt together; combine the two mixtures, blend thoroughly. Spread batter in a greased 13x9x2-inch pan. Sprinkle nuts, chocolate chips and marshmallows over the batter. Beat the 2 egg whites stiff; fold in brown sugar. Spread over top of cake. Bake 30-40 minutes in a 350° oven. Cut into bars.

Yield: 4 dozen

Brown-Sugar Chews

1 egg
1 cup brown sugar, packed
1 tsp. vanilla
½ cup flour
¼ tsp. salt
¼ tsp. soda
1 cup chopped walnuts

Beat egg, brown sugar and vanilla until well creamed. Sift together flour, salt and soda; add to creamed mixture. Add nuts. Bake 18 minutes in a well-greased 8x8x2-inch pan in a 350° oven.

Yield: 2½ dozen

Brown-Sugar Bars

½ cup dark brown sugar, packed
1 cup flour
½ cup melted butter
2 eggs
1 cup dark brown sugar, packed
1 cup chopped pecans
½ tsp. baking powder

Mix together ½ cup brown sugar, flour and butter, pat into greased 8x8x2-inch pan, bake 15 minutes in a 350° oven. Beat eggs well, add 1 cup brown sugar, pecans, baking powder and mix well, pour over the baked batter, return to oven and bake 20 minutes. Do *not* double recipe.

Yield: 2½ dozen

Chocolate-Chip Butterscotch Bars

½ cup butter
2 cups brown sugar
2 eggs, beaten
1 tsp. vanilla
1 Tblsp. milk
1½ cups flour
2 tsp. baking powder
½ tsp. salt
½ cup chocolate chips
½ cup chopped nuts

Melt butter over low heat. Remove from heat and add brown sugar, mixing well. Cool. Add beaten eggs, vanilla and milk to blend. Sift together flour, baking powder and salt; add with chips and nuts. Pour into a greased 13x9x2-inch pan and bake for 20-30 minutes in a 350° oven. Cool on rack and cut.

Yield: 4 dozen

Butterscotch Brownies

½ cup butter
2 cups brown sugar
2 eggs
1 tsp. vanilla
1½ cups flour
2 tsp. baking powder
1 cup chopped nuts (optional)

Melt butter over low heat, add sugar, bring to a boil stirring constantly. Cool to lukewarm, add eggs one at a time, beating well after each addition. Add vanilla. Sift together flour and baking powder; blend into mixture. Fold in nuts. Pour into greased and floured 11x7x2-inch pan and bake 30 minutes in a 350° oven. Cut when cool.

Yield: 3 dozen

Butterscotch Cheesecake Bars

12 oz. butterscotch chips
⅓ cup butter
2 cups graham cracker crumbs
1 cup chopped nuts
8 oz. cream cheese, softened
1 can sweetened condensed milk
1 tsp. vanilla
1 egg

Melt butterscotch chips and butter in saucepan; stir in crumbs and nuts. Press ½ of mixture firmly into bottom of greased 13x9x2-inch pan. Beat cream cheese until fluffy, add condensed milk, vanilla and egg, beating well. Pour into pan, top with remaining mixture of crumbs and nuts. Bake in a 350° oven for 25-30 minutes, or until tester comes out clean. Cool to room temperature before refrigerating. Best if made 24 hours in advance.

Yield: 4 dozen

Cheesecake Cookies

⅓ cup brown sugar, packed
½ cup chopped walnuts
1 cup flour
⅓ cup butter, melted
8 oz. cream cheese
¼ cup sugar
1 egg
1 Tblsp. lemon juice
2 Tblsp. cream or milk
1 tsp. vanilla

Blend brown sugar, walnuts and flour, then mix with butter until crumbly. Save 1 cup of mixture for topping. Place remainder in a lightly greased 8x8x2-inch pan. Press firmly. Bake at 350° for 12-15 minutes. Beat cream cheese and sugar until smooth; add egg, lemon juice, cream and vanilla. Pour this mixture into baked crust. Top with reserved crumbs. Return to 350° oven and bake about 25 minutes. Cool thoroughly before cutting. Store in refrigerator.

Yield: 2½ dozen

Peanut-Butter Oatmeal Bars

½ cup butter, softened
⅓ cup peanut butter
½ cup sugar
½ cup brown sugar, packed
1 egg, beaten
1 cup flour
½ tsp. soda
1 cup quick oatmeal

Cream together butter and peanut butter, add sugars and beaten egg; mix well. Thoroughly blend in flour, soda and oatmeal. Press dough into a greased 9x9x2-inch pan. Bake in a 350° oven for 20-25 minutes. Cut into bars.

Yield: 3 dozen

Chocolate Oatmeal Bars

½ cup sugar
½ cup brown sugar, packed
1 cup butter
1 tsp. vanilla
2 egg yolks
1 cup flour
1 cup quick oatmeal

Cream together sugars and butter. Add vanilla and egg yolks, mixing well. Stir in flour and oatmeal. Turn into an *ungreased* 15x10-inch jelly-roll pan. Bake 15-20 minutes in a 350° oven. Cool.

Topping:
8 oz. milk chocolate
2 Tblsp. butter
1 cup chopped nuts

Melt chocolate and butter, mix and spread on top. Sprinkle with nuts. Cut bars when cool.

Yield: 5 dozen

Chocolate Creme Squares

8 oz. cream cheese
1 can (5.33 oz.) evaporated milk
12 oz. chocolate chips
1 oz. unsweetened chocolate
pinch salt
2 cups flour + pinch salt
⅔ cup sugar
⅔ cup melted butter
½ tsp. vanilla
1 cup chopped walnuts

In a heavy saucepan combine cream cheese, evaporated milk, chocolate chips, chocolate and salt. Cook over low heat, stirring until smooth. In a food processor combine flour, salt, sugar, melted butter and vanilla, pulsing until crumbly. Remove 1¼ cups of crumbs for topping. Spread remainder in a greased foil-lined 13x9x2-inch pan. Spread chocolate over crumbs. Mix walnuts with 1¼ cups of crumbs and spread over chocolate mixture. Bake in a 325° oven for 25-30 minutes until lightly browned. Cool and cut.

Variation: Flavor with 1 Tblsp. rum *or* ½ tsp. almond extract *or* ½ tsp. peppermint, added to chocolate filling.

Yield: 4 dozen

Dream Bars

Crumb mixture:
½ cup butter
½ cup brown sugar, packed
1 cup flour

Mix ingredients to a crumbly mass. Pack firmly into a greased 12x8x2-inch pan. Bake for 10-15 minutes in a 350° oven. Meanwhile, prepare topping:

Topping:
2 eggs
1 cup brown sugar, packed
1 tsp. vanilla
2 Tblsp. flour
½ tsp. baking powder
¼ tsp. salt
1½ cups coconut
1 cup pecans

Beat eggs well, add 1 cup brown sugar and vanilla. Sift together flour, baking powder and salt; add to creamed mixture and blend well. Stir in coconut and pecans. Pour over baked crust and return to 350° oven for 20 minutes.

Yield: 3½ dozen

Walnut Bars

Crumb mixture:
½ cup butter, softened
½ cup brown sugar, packed
1 cup flour

Blend butter, sugar and flour. Pat evenly into 8x8x2-inch pan. Bake for 10-12 minutes in a 350° oven.

Filling:
2 eggs
1 cup brown sugar
3 Tblsp. flour
¼ tsp. salt
¼ tsp. baking powder
1 tsp. vanilla
1¼ cups chopped walnuts

Beat eggs until light. Add sugar gradually. Blend in sifted dry ingredients, vanilla and walnuts. Pour over crust. Return to 350° oven and bake for an additional 20 minutes. Cool and cut.

Yield: 2½ dozen

Frosted Praline Bars

1½ cups flour
1 tsp. baking powder
1 tsp. salt
½ cup butter
1½ cups brown sugar, packed
2 eggs
2 tsp. vanilla
¾ cup chopped pecans

Sift together flour, baking powder and salt; set aside. Melt butter, remove from heat and add brown sugar. Beat in eggs, one at a time; add vanilla and blend well. Add sifted dry ingredients, mixing well. Fold in pecans. Spread mixture in a greased 13x9x2-inch pan. Bake for 25-30 minutes in a 350° oven. Cool slightly in pan on rack. Prepare frosting.

Frosting:
2 Tblsp. butter
¼ cup brown sugar, packed
2 Tblsp. cream
1 cup confectioners' sugar

Combine butter, brown sugar and cream in saucepan. Cook until butter is melted; blend until smooth. Add confectioners' sugar, beat until consistency of frosting. Spread on warm bars.

Yield: 4 dozen

Bourbon Pecan Bars

1¼ cups flour
½ tsp. baking powder
½ tsp. salt
1 cup chopped toasted pecans
⅓ cup sugar
½ cup butter
3 eggs
1¼ cups brown sugar
¼ cup butter, melted and cooled
3 Tblsp. bourbon
1 tsp. vanilla
pinch salt

Sift together flour, baking powder and salt; add pecans, sugar and ½ cup cold butter, cut into pieces; blend mixture until it resembles meal. Press dough into a greased 9x9x2-inch pan and bake in a 350° oven for 15 minutes, or until it is golden brown. Beat eggs, 1¼ cups brown sugar, melted butter, bourbon, vanilla and salt until the mixture is well combined. Pour over baked layer, and bake in a 350° oven for 25 minutes, or until puffed and lightly browned. Cool and cut into squares.

Yield: 3 dozen

Butter-Pecan Bars

1 cup sweet butter
2½ cups flour
2 cups brown sugar, packed
2 eggs, beaten
1 tsp. vanilla
1½ tsp. baking powder
pinch salt
1 cup chopped pecans

Combine ½ cup of butter, 1¼ cups of flour and ⅓ cup sugar, press mixture on bottom of a greased and floured 13x9x2-inch pan. Bake for 15 minutes in a 350° oven. While crust is baking prepare filling. In a saucepan combine remaining sugar, butter and cook on low heat until melted; slowly stir into beaten eggs. Add vanilla. Sift together remaining flour, baking powder and salt; add with nuts. Pour over the crust, return to oven and bake for an additional 25 minutes. Allow to cool completely before cutting.

Yield: 3½ dozen

Date-Pecan Bars

1 cup flour
1 cup chopped dates
¾ cup sugar
½ cup butter, softened
½ tsp. cardamom
½ cup chopped pecans
2 eggs
1 tsp. baking powder
2 tsp. vanilla
½ tsp. salt

Combine all ingredients in 1½ quart mixing bowl. Stir by hand until mixed (1-2 minutes). Spread into greased 9x9x2-inch pan and bake in a 350° oven for 22-27 minutes, or until tester inserted in center comes out clean. Cool completely, cut into bars.

Yield: 3 dozen

Pecan Turtle Cookies

2 cups flour
1 cup brown sugar, packed
½ cup butter
1 cup whole pecan halves
⅔ cup butter
½ cup brown sugar, packed
1 cup milk chocolate chips

Mix flour, 1 cup brown sugar and ½ cup butter; blend well. Pat firmly into *ungreased* 13x9x2-inch pan. Place pecans evenly over unbaked crust. Combine ⅔ cup butter with ½ cup brown sugar in saucepan, cook over medium heat stirring constantly until mixture boils. Pour caramel layer over crust, bake 18-22 minutes in a 350° oven. Remove from oven and immediately sprinkle with chips, allow chips to melt slightly and swirl to achieve marbleized effect. Cool completely and cut.

Yield: 3½ dozen

Date-Nut Sticks

2 eggs
1 cup sugar
2 cups chopped nuts
4 oz. candied cherries, cut (optional)
16 oz. chopped dates
1 tsp. vanilla
few drops almond flavoring
½ cup flour
1 tsp. baking powder
confectioners' sugar

Cream eggs and sugar. Add nuts, cherries, dates, vanilla and almond flavoring. Add flour sifted with baking powder. Spread in greased 12x8x2-inch pan and bake in a 350° oven for about 30 minutes. Cool and cut in squares or strips. Sprinkle with confectioners' sugar.

Yield: 3½ dozen

Pecan Bars

1 cup flour
½ tsp. baking powder
⅓ cup dark brown sugar, packed
¼ cup butter
¼ cup dark brown sugar, packed
3 Tblsp. flour
2 eggs, beaten
¾ cup dark corn syrup
½ tsp. salt
1 tsp. vanilla
¾ cups pecans

Sift together first two ingredients. Stir in ⅓ cup brown sugar. Cut in butter, using pastry blender or food processor until blended (it will appear dry). Pat evenly in greased 12x8x2-inch pan and bake in a 350° oven for 10 minutes. Blend ¼ cup sugar and flour, set aside. Beat eggs, add corn syrup, flour mixture, salt and vanilla; mix well. Pour over partially baked batter, sprinkle with chopped nuts. Return to 350° oven for 25-30 minutes. Cut into bars while warm.

Yield: 3½ dozen

Honey Bars

½ cup butter
1 cup honey
1 tsp. vanilla
3 eggs
1¼ cups flour
1 tsp. baking powder
½ tsp. salt
1 cup chopped dates
1 cup chopped nuts
sugar

Cream butter, add honey, vanilla, eggs. Sift flour with baking powder and salt, mix with dates and nuts and add to creamed mixture. Spread batter into greased 13x9x2-inch pan and bake for 30-35 minutes in a 350° oven. Set on rack to cool, when cool cut in bars and roll in sugar.

Yield: 4 dozen

Zebras

1 cup butter, softened
1 cup brown sugar, packed
2 eggs
1 tsp. vanilla
2 cups flour
1 tsp. baking powder
1½ cups chocolate chips
¾ cup coarsely chopped walnuts

Cream butter and sugar until light and fluffy. Beat in eggs, one at time, beating well after each addition. Beat in vanilla. Stir in sifted flour and baking powder; blend well. Transfer half the batter to another bowl and mix in 1 cup *melted* chocolate chips. Spread chocolate mixture into a 13x9x2-inch greased pan which has been lined with foil, greased and floured. Drop spoonfuls of remaining batter over chocolate layer. Spread carefully. Sprinkle with remaining ½ cup chocolate chips and walnuts. Bake for 30-35 minutes in a 350° oven. Cool on rack.

Yield: 4 dozen

Snow-on-the-Mountain Bars

3 eggs
1 cup sugar
1 tsp. vanilla
¾ cup flour
1 tsp. baking powder
½ tsp. salt
2 cups chopped dates
1 cup chopped walnuts
confectioners' sugar

Beat eggs until thick and lemon-colored. Gradually add sugar, beating well. Blend in vanilla. Sift together flour, baking powder and salt. Stir dry ingredients into egg mixture, mixing well. Fold in dates and walnuts. Pour mixture into greased 13x9x2-inch pan. Bake in a 350° oven for 25 minutes. Cool in pan. Sprinkle with confectioners' sugar.

Yield: 4 dozen

ELIZABETH JOHANSSON (American, b. 1954)
Eggs in a Net Bag; graphite on paper, 1985
Gift of Stephen and Sybil Stone

Cranberry Spice Squares

1 cup cranberries (fresh or frozen)
2 cups flour
1 tsp. soda
½ tsp. salt
1 tsp cinnamon
1 tsp. cloves
1 tsp. nutmeg
½ cup butter, softened
1 cup brown sugar, packed
1 egg
1 cup milk

Chop cranberries coarsely. Set aside. Sift together flour, soda, salt, cinnamon, cloves and nutmeg. Cream butter with sugar and egg until light and fluffy. Add flour mixture alternately with milk. Mix just until combined. Stir in cranberries. Pour into a well-greased and floured 8x8x2-inch pan. Bake in a 350° oven 60-65 minutes, or until cake tester inserted in center comes out clean. Let cool in pan 10 minutes. Turn out on rack to cool completely. If desired, may be frosted before cut into squares.

Cranberry Cheese Frosting:
3 oz. cream cheese
2 Tblsp. jellied cranberry sauce
3½ cups confectioners' sugar

Beat cream cheese until light. Gradually beat in cranberry sauce, add confectioners' sugar, beating until smooth and fluffy.

Golden Apricot Bars

Crumb mixture:
1½ cups flour
½ cup brown sugar, packed
½ cup butter

Combine flour and sugar, cut in butter to prepare crumb mixture. Pat into a 13x9x2-inch greased pan and bake in a 275° oven for 10 minutes.

Filling:
¾ cup dried apricots, chopped
2 eggs, beaten
1 cup brown sugar, packed
½ tsp. vanilla
2 Tblsp. flour
½ tsp. baking powder
¼ tsp. salt

Soak apricots in hot water for 6-8 minutes, drain well. Beat eggs well, add sugar and vanilla. Stir in sifted dry ingredients. Fold chopped apricots into batter. Pour over baked pastry and bake an additional 20 minutes in a 350° oven. Frost with butter cream frosting, if desired.

Yield: 4 dozen

Apricot Squares

1 cup sugar
2½ cups flour
¾ cup butter
1⅓ cups coconut
½ cup chopped nuts
1 egg
1 tsp. vanilla
¼ tsp. salt
10-oz. jar apricot jam

Blend all ingredients except jam, mixture should resemble crumbs. Press one-half of mixture in greased 9x9x2-inch pan, spread with apricot jam and sprinkle with remaining crumb mixture. Bake for 35 minutes in a 350° oven until lightly browned. Cool and cut into squares.

Yield: 3 dozen

Apricot Oatmeal Bars

Crumb Mixture:
1¼ cups flour
½ cup sugar
½ tsp. soda
¼ tsp. salt
1¼ cups quick oatmeal
¾ cup melted butter
2 tsp. vanilla

Filling:
10 oz. apricot preserves *or* marmalade
½ cup flaked coconut *or* pecans

Combine all crumb mixture ingredients until mixture is crumbly (1-2 minutes), *reserve 1 cup crumb mixture:* press remaining crumb mixture into greased 13x9x2-inch pan. Spread apricot preserves to within ½″ from edge of unbaked crumb mixture, sprinkle with reserved crumb mixture and coconut. Bake near the center of a 350° oven for 25-30 minutes, or until edges are lightly browned.

Yield: 4 dozen

Raisin Mumbles

Filling:
2½ cups raisins
1 Tblsp. cornstarch
½ cup sugar
¾ cup water
3 Tblsp. lemon juice

Combine ingredients in saucepan and cook, stirring constantly over low heat until thick (about 5 minutes). Cool.

Crumb mixture:
¾ cup butter
1 cup brown sugar, packed
1¾ cups flour
½ tsp. soda
½ tsp. salt
1½ cups quick oatmeal

Cream butter and sugar; mix in dry ingredients, then oatmeal. Press half of mixture into greased 13x9x2-inch pan. Spread on raisin filling. Pat on remaining crumbs. Bake in a 400° oven for 20 minutes, or until nicely browned. Cut into squares.

Yield: 4 dozen

Variation: Date and Oatmeal Bars
Substitute 2 cups pitted dates, cut up, for raisins. Proceed as above.

Chocolate Raisin Bars

½ cup raisins
3 Tblsp. rum
½ cup flour
½ cup chopped walnuts
½ cup brown sugar, packed
¼ tsp. soda
¼ cup butter, melted and cooled
1 oz. unsweetened chocolate
¼ cup butter
½ cup brown sugar, packed
1 egg, beaten
¼ cup flour
⅛ tsp. cinnamon
⅛ tsp. allspice

Combine raisins and rum and macerate for 1 hour. Combine ½ cup flour, walnuts, ½ cup brown sugar, soda and melted butter, blend until mixture resembles coarse meal. Press dough into a greased 9x9x2-inch pan and bake in a 350° oven for 15 minutes, or until lightly browned. Melt chocolate and ¼ cup butter. Remove from heat, stir in ½ cup brown sugar and beat in egg. Stir in the raisins, ¼ cup flour, cinnamon and allspice. Pour mixture over baked crust and bake in 350° oven for 15 minutes, or until a tester comes out clean. Cool and cut.

Yield: 3 dozen

Prune Nut Bars

1 cup chopped prunes
1 cup apple, peeled and chopped
1/3 cup dry sherry
6 Tblsp. butter, softened
3/4 cup brown sugar, packed
1 egg, lightly beaten
1 tsp. vanilla
1 tsp. cinnamon
1/4 tsp. allspice
1/4 tsp. cloves
1/4 tsp. nutmeg
1/2 cup chopped walnuts
3/4 cup flour
1/2 tsp. baking powder
1/4 tsp. salt

Combine prunes, apples and 1/3 cup sherry; macerate for at least 2 hours. Cream together butter and brown sugar until the mixture is light and fluffy. Add egg, vanilla, cinnamon, allspice, cloves and nutmeg; combine and mix well. Stir in the apple, prune mixture and walnuts. Sift together flour, baking powder and salt, add and stir batter until just combined. Spoon batter into a greased 9x9x2-inch pan and bake in a 350° oven for 30-35 minutes, or until lightly brown. Cool and cut.

Yield: 3 dozen

Double Apple Bars

1/4 cup butter
1/2 cup + 2 Tblsp. brown sugar
1 egg
1 cup applesauce
2 cups diced, pared Golden Delicious apples
1 1/2 cups flour
1 tsp. cinnamon
1/2 tsp. baking powder
1/2 tsp. soda
1/4 tsp. cloves
1 1/2 cups chopped walnuts

Cream butter and 1/2 cup sugar until light and fluffy. Beat in egg, then applesauce (mixture will look curdled). Sift together flour, cinnamon, baking powder, soda and cloves; stir into creamed mixture. Fold in apples and 1/2 cup walnuts. Spread evenly in greased 13x9x2-inch pan. In a small bowl mix remaining 1 cup walnuts and 2 Tblsp. brown sugar; sprinkle over batter. Bake 35 minutes in a 375° oven until sides pull away and top is lightly browned. Cool on rack.

Yield: 4 dozen

Crunch-Top Applesauce Bars

1 cup sugar
1 cup applesauce, unsweetened
1/2 cup butter, softened
2 cups flour
1 tsp. soda
1 1/2 tsp. cinnamon
1 tsp. nutmeg
dash cloves
1/4 tsp. salt
1 cup raisins
1/4 cup chopped walnuts
1 tsp. vanilla
2/3 cup Cornflake crumbs
1/4 cup sugar
1/4 cup chopped walnuts
2 Tblsp. butter, softened

Combine sugar and applesauce. Add butter and blend. Sift together flour, soda, spices and salt. Add to applesauce mixture and stir until smooth. Stir in raisins, nuts and vanilla. Spread batter in a greased 15x10-inch jelly-roll pan. Combine Cornflakes, sugar, nuts and butter. Sprinkle over top of batter. Bake in a 350° oven for 20-25 minutes, or until done. Cool and cut into bars.

Yield: 5 dozen

Fresh Apple-Cake Bars

2 cups sugar
2 cups flour
2 Tblsp. soda
1 tsp. salt
2 tsp. cinnamon
2 tsp. nutmeg
2 eggs, beaten
2 tsp. vanilla
1 cup vegetable oil
3 cups chopped apples, *unpeeled*
1 cup raisins

Sift together first six ingredients. In a large bowl beat eggs, add vanilla and oil; blend well. Combine with dry ingredients. Add apples and raisins. Press into *ungreased* 17x12x2-inch pan and bake in a 350° oven for 35-40 minutes. Cut into squares.

Yield: 7 dozen

Sour-Cream Apple Squares

2 cups flour
2 cups brown sugar, packed
½ cup butter, softened
1 cup chopped nuts
1½ tsp. cinnamon
1 tsp. soda
½ tsp. salt
1 cup sour cream
1 tsp. vanilla
1 egg
2 cups finely chopped apples

In a large bowl, combine flour, brown sugar and butter; blend at low speed just until crumbly. Stir in nuts. Press 2¾ cups crumb mixture into *ungreased* 13x9x2-inch pan. To remaining mixture, add cinnamon, soda, salt, sour cream, vanilla and egg; blend well. Stir in apples. Spoon evenly over base. (If desired sprinkle ½ cup nuts over top.) Bake in a 350° oven for 25-30 minutes.

Yield: 4 dozen

Apple Brownies

½ cup butter
1 cup sugar
1 egg
1 cup flour
¾ tsp. cinnamon
½ tsp. soda
½ tsp. baking powder
2 cups chopped nuts
confectioners' sugar

Cream butter and sugar, add egg. Sift together flour, cinnamon, soda and baking powder; add to creamed mixture. Stir in apples and nuts. Spread in greased 9x9x2-inch pan. Bake about 40 minutes in a 350° oven. Cool and cut in squares. If desired, dust with confectioners' sugar before cutting.

Yield: 3 dozen

Chocolate Applesauce Bars

½ cup butter
2 oz. unsweetened chocolate
2 eggs
1 cup brown sugar, packed
1 tsp. vanilla
½ cup applesauce
1 cup flour
½ tsp. baking powder
¼ tsp. soda
¼ tsp. salt
½ cup chopped walnuts

Combine butter and chocolate in saucepan over low heat, stirring until melted. Remove and cool slightly. Combine eggs, brown sugar and vanilla, beat until well blended. Add chocolate mixture and applesauce. Sift together flour, baking powder, soda and salt. Gradually stir in dry ingredients, mixing well. Fold in walnuts. Pour mixture into greased 13x9x2-inch pan. Bake for 25 minutes in 350° oven until top springs back when touched lightly.

Yield: 4 dozen

Raisin Toffee Bars

1 cup flour
½ tsp. salt
½ cup butter, softened
1 cup brown sugar, packed
1 tsp. vanilla
2 eggs
2 cups bran flakes
1 cup raisins

Sift together flour and salt; set aside. Combine butter and sugar, mix thoroughly. Add vanilla and eggs. Beat well. Stir in bran flakes and raisins. Add flour mixture; stir until thoroughly combined. Spread in well-greased 9x9x2-inch pan. Bake for 30 minutes in a 350° oven, or until well done. Cool in pan on rack. Frost. Let stand until set.

Icing:
1 cup confectioners' sugar
1 Tblsp. butter, softened
½ tsp. vanilla
1 or 2 Tblsp. milk

Beat until smooth and spread over bars.

Yield: 3 dozen

Chewy Crumb Bars

1 cup bread crumbs, fine dry
1 cup sugar
½ cup chopped walnuts
½ cup chopped raisins
2 eggs, beaten
¼ cup milk

Combine bread crumbs, sugar, chopped nuts and raisins. Add eggs and milk. Mix well. Pour into a greased 11x7x2-inch pan. Bake in a 350° oven for 25-30 minutes. Cut in bars while hot. Cool before removing from pan.

Yield: 3 dozen

Hermits

¼ cup vegetable oil
½ cup butter
1 cup sugar
1 egg
¼ cup molasses
2¼ cups flour
2 tsp. soda
¼ tsp. salt
¾ tsp. ginger
1 tsp. cinnamon
¾ tsp. cloves
1 cup raisins
sugar

Cream together shortenings and sugar. Add egg, then molasses, blending well after each addition. Sift all dry ingredients together and stir into the creamed mixture. Add raisins. Pour batter in an *ungreased* 17x12-inch jelly-roll pan and press. Sprinkle sugar over dough and bake for 10 minutes in a 375° oven.

Yield: 6 dozen

Lebkuchen

4 eggs
2 cups flour
¾ cup raisins
1 lb. dark brown sugar
1 Tblsp. cinnamon

Combine ingredients and mix well. Bake in a greased 10x15-inch jelly-roll pan in a 375° oven for 20 minutes. Do not overcook. While hot, spread with glaze of confectioners' sugar and lemon juice (dark rum can be substituted, if desired). Store well covered (improves with age).

Yield: 5 dozen

Holiday Lebkuchen

2¾ cups flour
½ tsp. soda
1 tsp. cinnamon
½ tsp. nutmeg
½ tsp. cloves
½ cup finely chopped nuts
½ cup finely chopped candied mixed fruit
1 egg, slightly beaten
1 cup dark corn syrup
¾ cup brown sugar, packed
1 Tblsp. lemon juice
1 tsp. grated lemon peel

Sift together flour, soda and spices, stir in nuts and candied fruit, set aside. Beat egg and add corn syrup, sugar, lemon juice and peel; mix well. Stir in flour-fruit mixture. Divide dough in half and turn out on well-greased and floured cookie baking sheets. Moisten hand and flatten dough to ⅛″ thickness (dough will rise during baking). Bake in a 400° oven for 12-15 minutes, or until lightly browned and firm to the touch. Remove from oven and immediately brush with thin icing made with confectioners' sugar and lemon juice; decorate with holiday sprinkles. Cut into bars while still warm. Cover tightly and store until mellow.

Yield: 5 dozen

Frosted Ginger Diamonds

½ cup butter
½ cup brown sugar, packed
1 egg, beaten
2 cups flour
½ tsp. salt
1 tsp. ginger
¼ tsp. cloves
1 tsp. cinnamon
½ tsp. nutmeg
½ cup molasses
⅔ cup buttermilk
1 cup raisins, chopped fine

Cream butter and sugar, add beaten egg and mix thoroughly. Sift dry ingredients together, add ⅓ of the dry ingredients to the creamed mixture. Add molasses, then another ⅓ dry ingredients. Beat well. Add milk, blend; add balance dry ingredients and raisins. Stir well and spread batter ¼″ thick on 2 lightly greased large baking sheets. Bake in a 350° oven for 15 minutes. Cool slightly and frost.

Frosting:
2 Tblsp. butter
1½ cups confectioners' sugar
2 Tblsp. hot coffee

Cream butter and confectioners' sugar. Add hot coffee and mix to spreading consistency. Spread on warm cookies in pan. Cut in diamonds.

Yield: 6 dozen

Fruitcake Bars

½ cup chopped walnuts
1 cup raisins
1 cup chopped dates
1 cup candied fruit (no citron)
½ cup flour
4 eggs
1 cup brown sugar
½ tsp. salt
1 tsp. vanilla
1 tsp. lemon/orange juice
1 tsp. grated lemon/orange peel

Toss walnuts and fruits with flour. Set aside. Beat eggs and sugar with salt, vanilla, lemon juice and peel. Stir in flour mixture. Spread in greased 15x10-inch jelly-roll pan. Bake in a 325° oven for 30 minutes.

Yield: 5 dozen

JOHN SINGLETON COPLEY (American, 1738–1815)
Paul Revere; oil painting, 1768–1770
Gift of Joseph W., William B., and Edward H. R. Revere

Orange Squares

2 Tblsp. butter
½ cup sugar
2 eggs
⅔ cup orange marmalade
1 cup bran flakes
⅔ cup flour
1 tsp. salt
1 tsp. baking powder
½ cup chopped blanched almonds

Thoroughly cream butter and sugar. Add eggs, marmalade and bran flakes. Mix well. Add sifted dry ingredients and almonds; mix thoroughly. Pour into greased 8x8x2-inch pan and bake for 30 minutes in a 375° oven.

Yield: 2½ dozen

Love Lemon Bars

1 cup butter
2 cups flour
½ cup confectioners' sugar
4 eggs
2 cups sugar
¼ cup flour
1 tsp. baking powder
6 Tblsp. fresh lemon juice
grated peel of 1 lemon
confectioners' sugar

Blend butter, 2 cups flour and confectioners' sugar thoroughly. Press dough into a well-greased and floured 13x9x2-inch pan. Bake for 25 minutes in a 350° oven. Watch closely. Beat eggs until frothy. Add all remaining ingredients and beat until smooth. Pour into the crust and bake 20-25 minutes at 350°. Dust with confectioners' sugar and cut into squares. Refrigerate.

Variation for filling:
4 eggs
2 cups sugar
5 Tblsp. fresh lemon juice
1 tsp. baking powder
dash salt

Mix well and pour over baked crust. Bake for 20-25 minutes in a 350° oven.

Yield: 4 dozen

Golden Lemon Bars

Crumb mixture:
1½ cups flour
½ cup brown sugar, packed
½ cup butter

Combine flour and brown sugar; cut in butter and pat mixture in greased 13x9x2-inch pan. Bake 10 minutes in a 375° oven.

Filling:
2 eggs
1 cup brown sugar
½ tsp. vanilla
2 Tblsp. flour
½ tsp. baking powder
1¼ cups coconut
½ cup chopped pecans

Beat eggs well, add brown sugar and vanilla; blend thoroughly. Add flour, baking powder, coconut and pecans. Pour over hot crust. Bake an additional 20 minutes at 350°. Remove from oven and immediately spread glaze.

Lemon Glaze:
1 cup confectioners' sugar
1½ Tblsp. butter
2-3 tsp. lemon juice
1 tsp. grated lemon peel

Combine all ingredients and blend well until smooth.

Yield: 4 dozen

Lemon Coconut Bars

1½ cups grated, sweetened coconut
1 cup flour
½ cup cold butter, cut
¼ cup sugar
3 eggs
1 cup sugar
⅓ cup fresh lemon juice
1 Tblsp. grated lemon peel
1 Tblsp. flour
⅛ tsp. salt
confectioners' sugar

Combine coconut, 1 cup flour and butter, cut into pieces; add ¼ cup sugar and blend until mixture resembles meal. Press dough into a well-greased 9x9x2-inch pan and bake in a 350° oven for 15 minutes, or until golden brown. Beat eggs, 1 cup sugar, lemon juice, lemon peel, flour and salt until mixture is well combined. Pour over the baked layer and bake in a 350° oven for 35 minutes, or until filling is set. Sift confectioners' sugar over top. Cool and cut.

Yield: 3 dozen

Lemon Almond Bars

Crumb mixture:
¼ cup confectioners' sugar
1 cup flour
2 Tblsp. finely ground almonds
½ cup butter

Mix together sugar, flour, almonds and butter until well blended. Press into a greased 9x9x2-inch pan. Bake in a 350° oven for 18 minutes.

Filling:
2 eggs, lightly beaten
1 Tblsp. lemon juice
grated peel of 1 lemon
1 cup sugar
2 Tblsp. flour
½ tsp. baking powder
½ cup sliced almonds, toasted

Lightly beat eggs. Add lemon juice, lemon peel, sugar, flour and baking powder, mix until thoroughly blended. Pour on top of baked crust. Top with ½ cup sliced, toasted almonds. Bake for 25 minutes in 350° oven.

Yield: 3 dozen

Lemon Crunch

Crumb mixture:
½ cup butter
½ cup brown sugar, packed
½ cup flour

Cream together butter, brown sugar and flour. Spread in 13x9x2-inch greased pan. Bake in a 375° oven for 12 minutes.

Filling:
2 eggs, beaten
1 cup brown sugar, packed
1 tsp. vanilla
½ cup flour
½ tsp. salt
1½ cups coconut
¾ cup chopped nuts

Beat eggs, add sugar and vanilla; beat until well blended. Add flour, salt, coconut and nuts. Spoon over first layer, carefully spreading. Bake in a 375° oven for 20 minutes.

Icing:
1½ cups confectioners' sugar
2 Tblsp. lemon juice

Mix sugar and lemon juice to creamy consistency and spread over hot mixture.

Lemon Currant Bars

⅓ cup dark currants
2 tsp. grated lemon peel
2½ Tblsp. fresh lemon juice
½ cup butter, softened
1 cup confectioners' sugar
1 egg
1½ cups flour
½ tsp. baking powder

Marinate currants, lemon peel and juice for 15 minutes; set aside. Cream butter and sugar, add egg and currant mixture. Sift together flour and baking powder; add and stir until blended. Spread batter in 11x7x2-inch pan that has been greased, lined with foil, greased and floured. Bake in a 350° oven for 25 minutes or until top is lightly browned and edges pull away. Cool in pan on rack overnight before cutting.

Yield: 3 dozen

Lemon Sticks

½ cup butter
½ cup confectioners' sugar
2 eggs, separated
1 cup flour
2 tsp. grated lemon peel
½ cup sugar
1 Tblsp. lemon juice
½ cup chopped walnuts

Cream butter, gradually adding confectioners' sugar. Add egg yolks, beat until light. Stir in flour and lemon peel. Mix until smooth and spread evenly in bottom of *ungreased* 13x9x2-inch pan. Bake 10 minutes in a 350° oven. While this is baking, beat egg whites stiff, gradually adding sugar. Beat in lemon juice and fold in nuts. Spread meringue topping over baked mixture and bake 25 minutes longer. Cool slightly and cut.

Yield: 4 dozen

Strawberry Almond Bars

1 cup flour
½ cup + 3 Tblsp. sugar
½ cup cold butter, cut in ½-inch pieces
¾ cup strawberry jam
2 egg whites at room temperature
2 cups sliced unblanched almonds

Put flour and ½ cup sugar in food processor, cut in butter until crumbly. Grease a 13x9x2-inch pan, line with foil and grease foil. Press crumbs evenly in bottom. Bake in a 350° oven for 15 minutes until firm and lightly browned. Cool in pan on rack and spread with jam. Beat eggs whites until soft peaks form, slowly add remaining 3 Tblsp. sugar, beat until shiny. Fold in 1 cup almonds and drop mixture on bottom layer, sprinkle remaining 1 cup almonds on top. Bake for 25-30 minutes in 350° oven until lightly browned and top is set. Cool in pan on rack.

Yield: 4 dozen

Mincemeat Bars

2 cups quick oatmeal
1¾ cups flour
½ tsp. soda
½ cup ground nuts (optional)
1 cup brown sugar
1 cup butter
1½ cups moist mincemeat

Mix together oatmeal, flour, soda, nuts and sugar, cut in butter with pastry blender or food processor. Press ½ mixture firmly into bottom of a 11x7x2-inch greased pan. Spread mincemeat evenly on top. Cover with balance of mixture on top and pat down. Bake for 40 minutes in a 350° oven. Cool and cut into bars.

Yield: 3 dozen

Carrot Bars

2 eggs
1 cup sugar
¾ cup vegetable oil
1 jar junior baby food carrots
1 tsp. vanilla
1¼ cups flour
1 tsp. soda
½ tsp. salt
1 tsp. cinnamon
½ cup nuts, broken pieces
½ cup raisins

Beat eggs, add sugar and oil; beat well. Add carrots and vanilla. Stir in sifted dry ingredients, nuts and raisins. Grease and flour a 13x9x2-inch pan. Bake in a 350° oven for 25 minutes. Cool and frost.

Frosting:
1½ cups confectioners' sugar
¼ cup butter
3 oz. cream cheese
1 tsp. vanilla

Beat well and spread.

Yield: 4 dozen

Pumpkin Bars

4 eggs
1 cup vegetable oil
2 cups sugar
1 cup pumpkin
½ tsp. salt
1 tsp. soda
2 cups flour
2 tsp. cinnamon
1 tsp. baking powder
½ cup nuts, chopped
½ cup raisins

Beat eggs well, add oil and sugar, continue beating until thoroughly blended. Add pumpkin. Sift together dry ingredients and stir into pumpkin mixture. Add nuts and raisins. Pour into a greased, floured 17x12-inch jelly-roll pan and bake in a 350° oven for 20-25 minutes. Frost bars while still warm.

Frosting:
3 oz. cream cheese, softened
6 Tblsp. butter, softened
¾ cup confectioners' sugar
1 tsp. vanilla
1 tsp. milk

Cream together cream cheese and butter, gradually add sugar and vanilla. Add enough milk to make frosting spreading consistency.

Yield: 6 dozen

Sour-Cream Rhubarb Squares

½ cup sugar
½ cup chopped nuts
1 Tblsp. butter, melted
1 tsp. cinnamon
¾ cup brown sugar, packed
½ cup butter
1 egg
1 cup flour
1 tsp. soda
¼ tsp. salt
1 cup quick oatmeal
1 cup sour cream
1½ cups rhubarb (½″ pieces)

Mix sugar, nuts, melted butter and cinnamon; set aside. Cream together brown sugar, ½ cup butter and egg. Thoroughly stir together flour, soda, salt and oatmeal. Add to creamed mixture alternately with sour cream. Stir in rhubarb. Turn into greased 13x9x2-inch pan. Sprinkle with reserved topping. Bake for 45 minutes in a 350° oven.

Glaze:

Make glaze with confectioners' sugar, dash of cinnamon and thinned with milk to a consistency of light cream. Drizzle glaze over top while still warm.

Yield: 4 dozen

DAVID DAVISON (American, b. 1942)
Teapot; porcelain, 1976
Gift of Mr. and Mrs. Stephen D. Paine

Pumpkin Nut Bars

½ cup butter
¾ cup brown sugar
¾ cup flour
½ tsp. soda
½ tsp. baking powder
1 tsp. cinnamon
¼ tsp. ginger
¼ tsp. nutmeg
⅔ cup pumpkin
2 eggs
1 tsp. vanilla
½ cup chopped nuts

Combine all ingredients except nuts in a large bowl; beat well until thoroughly blended. Fold in nuts. Spread evenly on a greased and floured 13x9x2-inch pan. Bake about 20 minutes in a 250° oven. Cool. Frost with 1¼ cups confectioners' sugar, 2 Tblsp. butter and 2 Tblsp. orange juice; blend until smooth.

Yield: 4 dozen

Magic Hello Dollies

½ cup butter
1 cup graham cracker crumbs
1 cup coconut
6 oz. chocolate chips
6 oz. butterscotch chips
1 can sweetened condensed milk
1 cup chopped pecans

Melt butter in 12x8x2-inch pan in oven. Sprinkle crumbs over butter, then pat down. Sprinkle on coconut, chocolate chips and butterscotch chips. Do not mix, just sprinkle one ingredient over the other. Drizzle milk over all. Top with chopped pecans. Bake for 25-30 minutes in a 350° oven. Do not overbake. Cool in pan before cutting into bars.

Yield: 3½ dozen

Candy-Bar Cookies

Bars:
⅔ cup butter
½ cup light corn syrup
1 cup brown sugar, packed
4 cups quick oatmeal

Thoroughly grease a 15x10-inch jelly-roll pan. Mix all ingredients well. Bake in a 350° oven for 15 minutes. Cool slightly.

Topping:
6 oz. chocolate chips
2 cups crunchy peanut butter

Melt chocolate chips, add crunchy peanut butter, spread on cookie base, cut while warm.

Yield: 5 dozen

Cashew-Caramel Yummies

2 eggs, beaten
½ cup sugar
½ cup brown sugar, packed
¾ cup flour
½ tsp. baking powder
¼ tsp. salt
½ cup chopped salted cashews

Beat eggs, gradually mix in sugars. Sift together dry ingredients; stir into first mixture. Fold in cashews. Spread in well-greased 9x9x2-inch pan. Bake in a 350° oven for 25-30 minutes. Cover with cashew topping.

Cashew Topping:
2 Tblsp. butter, melted
¼ cup brown sugar, packed
1½ Tblsp. cream
⅓ cup chopped salted cashews

Combine butter, sugar and cream. Add cashews. Spread over hot bars and place under broiler until topping bubbles and is lightly brown, 1-3 minutes. Cut in squares while warm. Cool in pan.

Yield: 3 dozen

Oatmeal Carmelitas

Crumb mixture:
1 cup flour
1 cup oatmeal
¾ cup brown sugar
½ tsp. soda
¼ tsp. salt
½ cup melted butter

Combine all ingredients for crust. Blend well to form crumbs. Press half of crumbs into bottom of a greased 9x9x2-inch pan. Bake in a 350° oven for 10 minutes.

Filling:
6 oz. chocolate chips
½ cup chopped pecans
¾ cup caramel ice cream topping
3 Tblsp. flour

Sprinkle chocolate chips and pecans over baked crust. Blend caramel topping and flour, spread over chocolate and pecans. Sprinkle with remaining crumb mixture. Bake 15-20 minutes longer or until golden brown. Chill 1-2 hours. Cut into squares.

Yield: 3 dozen

Jeweled Cookies

2 eggs
1 cup sugar
1 tsp. vanilla
1 cup flour
½ tsp. salt
½ cup cut-up toasted almonds
¾ cup cut-up gumdrops (¼″)

Beat eggs until foamy. Beat in sugar and vanilla. Sift together and stir in flour and salt. Mix in nuts and ¼ cup gumdrops. Spread in a well-greased and floured 9x9x2-inch pan. Sprinkle ½ cup cut-up gumdrops over top of batter. Bake in a 325° oven for 30-35 minutes, until top has a dull crust. Cut into squares while warm. Cool. Remove from pan. Crust will crack.

Yield: 3 dozen

Caramel Rocky-Road Bars

Crumb mixture:
1 cup flour
½ tsp. soda
¼ tsp. salt
¾ cup quick oatmeal
½ cup sugar
½ cup butter
¼ cup chopped peanuts

Combine all ingredients except peanuts; beat 2 minutes. Stir in peanuts. Reserve ¾ cup of mixture; set aside. Press remaining crumb mixture into a greased and floured 9x9x2-inch pan. Bake in a 350° oven for 15 minutes, or until lightly browned.

Filling:
½ cup caramel topping
1½ cups miniature marshmallows
½ cup salted peanuts
½ cup milk chocolate pieces

Spread caramel topping evenly over hot crust. Sprinkle with marshmallows, peanuts, chocolate pieces and ¾ cup of crumb mixture. Return to oven for 20 minutes, until top is lightly browned. Cover, chill 3 hours, cut into bars. Cover and store in refrigerator.

Yield: 3 dozen

English Toffee Squares

1 cup brown sugar, packed
2 cups flour
¼ tsp. salt
1 cup butter
1 egg yolk
1 tsp. vanilla *or* ½ tsp. almond extract
6 oz. chocolate chips
½ cup chopped nuts

Mix dry ingredients, cut in butter. Add egg yolk and vanilla. Spread in greased 15x10-inch jelly-roll pan and bake for 15 minutes in 350° oven. Melt chocolate chips and spread over cookies, sprinkle with nuts.

Yield: 5 dozen

Toffee Bars

½ cup butter
1 cup brown sugar, packed
2 eggs
1 tsp. vanilla
1½ cups flour
1 tsp. salt
1 Tblsp. baking powder
1 cup chopped Heath Bars
½ cup chopped nuts

Cream butter, add sugar, eggs and vanilla. Sift together flour, salt and baking powder; blend with creamed mixture. Stir in Heath Bar pieces and chopped nuts. Bake in a greased 13x9x2-inch pan for 25 minutes in a 350° oven.

Yield: 4 dozen

Toasted-Pecan Toffee Bars

Bars:
2 cups flour
1 cup brown sugar, packed
½ tsp. cinnamon
1 cup butter
1 tsp. vanilla
¾ cup chopped pecans, toasted
½ cup milk-chocolate pieces

Topping:
½ cup milk-chocolate pieces
¼ cup chopped pecans

Combine flour, brown sugar, cinnamon, butter and vanilla until mixture is crumbly. Stir in ¾ cup pecans and ½ cup milk chocolate pieces. Press into greased 13x9x2-inch pan and bake for 25-30 minutes in a 350° oven, until edges are browned. Remove from oven and sprinkle with chocolate pieces, let stand 5 minutes and swirl chocolate pieces as they melt, do not spread, sprinkle with ¼ cup pecans. Cool completely and cut.

Yield: 4 dozen

Praline Grahams

½ cup butter
½ cup margarine
½ cup sugar
1 tsp. vanilla
1 cup chopped nuts
12 whole graham crackers

Melt together butter, margarine and sugar. Boil 2 minutes, add vanilla. Meanwhile, break graham crackers into fingers along stamped impressions and line greased 15x10-inch jelly-roll pan. Sprinkle nuts over crackers. Pour sugar and butter mixture over crackers. Bake in a 350° oven for 10 minutes. Place on rack to cool and separate while warm.

Yield: 4 dozen fingers

Chocolate Graham Bars

1 can sweetened condensed milk
2 cups crushed graham crackers
1 cup chocolate chips
½ cup coconut
½ cup chopped walnuts
1 tsp. vanilla
1 Tblsp. cocoa

Combine all ingredients. Mix well. Pour into greased 8x8x2-inch pan, bake in a 350° oven for 25 minutes, do not overbake. Cool and cut in squares. If desired, sprinkle with confectioners' sugar.

Yield: 2½ dozen

MIURA KENYA (Japanese, 1821–1889)
Tea caddy *(natsume)*; stoneware with enameled decoration
Edward Sylvester Morse Collection

Cinnamon Crunchies

1 cup flour
¼ tsp. salt
¼ tsp. cinnamon
⅓ cup butter
½ cup sugar
1 egg, separated
2 Tblsp. milk
¼ tsp. vanilla
3 Tblsp. sugar
¼ tsp. cinnamon
¼ cup chopped walnuts

Sift together flour, salt and cinnamon; set aside. Cream together butter and sugar, beat in egg yolk, milk, vanilla. Add dry ingredients, mix well. Spread batter in *ungreased* 11x7x2-inch pan. Beat egg white slightly and spread over surface of dough. Combine 3 Tblsp. sugar, cinnamon and walnuts, sprinkle over top. Bake for 30 minutes in a 350° oven. Cut in bars while still warm.

Yield: 3 dozen

Amaretto Cakes

1 cup butter
1 cup sugar
5 eggs, separated
½ cup flour
10 Amaretto cookies, finely crumbled
4 oz. semi-sweet chocolate, grated

Cream butter and sugar, add egg yolks, one at a time. Beat well. Gradually add flour and Amaretto cookie crumbs. Fold in *grated* chocolate. Beat egg whites stiff and fold into mixture. Bake in a greased 9x9x2-inch pan for 45 minutes in a 350° oven.

Yield: 3 dozen

Mound Bars

2 cups graham cracker crumbs
½ cup sugar
½ cup butter
2 cups flaked coconut
1 can sweetened condensed milk
1 tsp. vanilla
6 oz. chocolate chips, melted

Mix graham cracker crumbs, sugar and butter. Put mixture in a 13x9x2-inch pan. Combine coconut, milk and vanilla; place on top of crumbs. Bake 15 minutes in a 350° oven. Melt chocolate chips and spread on top of baked bars.

Yield: 4 dozen

Choco-Peanut Breakaways

1 cup butter, softened
1½ cups brown sugar, packed
¼ cup dark corn syrup
2 cups flour
6 oz. chocolate chips
1 cup salted peanuts
1 egg

Cream butter and sugar. Stir in remaining ingredients. Spread in greased 15x10-inch jelly-roll pan and bake in a 375° oven 20-25 minutes, do not overbake. Cool. Cut while warm, into squares, or cool and break away pieces.

Yield: 5 dozen

Coconut-Nut Bars

½ cup butter
2 cups brown sugar, packed
2 eggs
2 tsp. vanilla
1 cup flour, *unsifted*
2 tsp. baking powder
1 tsp. salt
1½ cups flaked coconut
½ cup chopped nuts

Melt butter. Remove from heat and combine with sugar, eggs and vanilla; mix well. Sift together flour, baking powder and salt; add to butter and sugar mixture, mixing well. Stir in coconut and nuts. Spread in a well-greased 13x9x2-inch pan. Bake for 20-30 minutes in a 350° oven. Cool and cut into squares.

Yield: 4 dozen

Scottish Butter Cookies

1 cup sweet butter, softened
⅔ cup sugar
2 cups flour
2 tsp. vanilla
¼ tsp. salt
confectioners' sugar

Cream butter with sugar until smooth. Gradually blend in flour, vanilla and salt; mix thoroughly. Pat mixture evenly into an *ungreased* 15x10-inch jelly-roll pan. Sprinkle top with powdered sugar. Bake in a 350° oven until golden, about 16-18 minutes. Cool 5 minutes, cut into squares while warm. Store in air-tight container.

Yield: 5 dozen

Dutch Butter Bars

½ cup butter
¾ cup sugar
1 egg, separated
1 tsp. lemon extract
2 cups sifted cake flour
chopped nuts

Combine butter, sugar, egg yolk, lemon extract and cake flour, mix thoroughly. Pat into a greased 15x10-inch jelly-roll pan, brush top with egg white and sprinkle with nuts. Bake for 15-20 minutes in a 350° oven. Cut in squares while warm.

Yield: 5 dozen

Drop Cookies

Drop cookies are made from a soft dough dropped from a teaspoon onto a greased cookie sheet. The cookies will have a better shape if a second spoon is used to push the dough off the first spoon so as to make uniform rounded cookies of the same size. Allow adequate space between mounds of dough so cookies can spread.

Bake until cookies are lightly browned and a slight imprint remains when touched gently with finger. Drop cookies should be fine, even in texture, tender, and slightly moist.

The batter for curled wafers should be quite thin, so cookie will spread. Remove wafers from a well-greased or foil-lined cookie sheet, cool a minute, and shape into desired curlform while hot and limp. Cookies become crisp when cool.

Coconut Snowdrops

½ cup sugar
1 cup butter, softened
1 egg
¼ cup milk
1 Tblsp. vanilla
2 cups flour
1 cup flaked coconut
confectioners' sugar

Cream butter and sugar; add egg and beat. Stir in milk, vanilla, flour and coconut; blend to combine. Drop by teaspoonfuls 2 inches apart onto *ungreased* cookie sheets. Bake 12-15 minutes in a 350° oven. Cool completely; sprinkle with confectioners' sugar.

Yield: 3 dozen

Date Macaroons

4 egg whites
1½ cups sugar
⅛ tsp. salt
1 tsp. vanilla
1 lb. pitted dates, chopped
1 cup chopped pecans

Beat egg whites until stiff, but not dry. Add sugar and salt gradually, continue beating until mixture holds shape. Blend in vanilla, fold in dates and nuts. Drop from teaspoon on greased cookie sheet, bake 20 minutes in a 350° oven.

Yield: 8 dozen

Angel Kisses

4 egg whites
⅛ tsp. cream of tartar
dash salt
1¼ cups confectioners' sugar *or* 1 cup sugar
½ tsp. vanilla

Beat egg whites stiff, gradually add cream of tartar, salt, sugar and vanilla. Drop by tablespoonful onto brown paper or foil lined cookie sheet. Bake in a 250° oven for 50 minutes.

Yield: 4 dozen

Cornflake Meringoons

2 egg whites
¼ tsp. salt
1 cup confectioners' sugar
¼ tsp. almond extract
1 cup shredded coconut
2 cups Cornflakes
6 oz. chocolate chips

Beat egg whites and salt until stiff. Slowly beat in sugar, add almond extract. Fold in coconut, Cornflakes and chocolate chips. Drop by teaspoonfuls onto a greased cookie sheet. Bake in a 350° oven for 25 minutes.

Yield: 3 dozen

JOSEPH RODEFER DECAMP (American, 1858–1923)
The Blue Cup; oil painting, 1909
Gift of Edwin S. Webster, Lawrence J. Webster, and
Mary S. Sampson in Memory of their Father, Frank G. Webster

French Nut Drops

2 egg whites
1 cup sugar
1 cup finely chopped walnuts
1 cup finely chopped pecans

Beat egg whites until stiff, but not dry. Gradually add sugar until thoroughly blended and holds shape. Stir in all of the finely chopped nuts. Put mixture in top of double boiler over boiling water and stir for 8 minutes, or until hot and slightly thickened. Cool, stirring several times, until cool enough to handle. Drop from teaspoon onto cookie sheet covered with brown paper. Bake in a 350° oven about 15 minutes, or until lightly browned. Allow drops to remain on paper about 1 minute before removing with spatula. Place on rack to cool.

Yield: 4 dozen

Chocolate Meringues

3 egg whites
pinch salt
1 cup sugar
6 oz. chocolate chips
2 Tblsp. cocoa
½ tsp. vanilla

Beat egg whites with salt until stiff. Gradually beat in sugar. Fold in chocolate chips, cocoa and vanilla. Drop batter, walnut-sized spoonfuls, onto foil-lined cookie sheets. Bake in a 275° oven for 30 minutes. Transfer entire foil sheet to rack and allow cookies to cool. Store in airtight container.

Yield: 4 dozen

Beacon Hill Cookies

6 oz. chocolate chips
2 egg whites
dash salt
½ cup sugar
½ tsp. vinegar
½ tsp. vanilla
¾ cup chopped nuts

Melt chocolate chips over hot water; set aside. Beat egg whites with salt until foamy. Gradually beat in sugar until it forms stiff peaks; beat in vinegar and vanilla. Fold in melted chocolate and nuts. Drop by teaspoonfuls on greased baking sheet, bake in a 350° oven for 10 minutes. Remove immediately.

Yield: 3 dozen

Coconut-Oatmeal Macaroons

2 cups flour
2½ tsp. baking powder
1 tsp. soda
1 tsp. salt
1 cup butter
2 cups brown sugar, packed
2 eggs
1½ tsp. vanilla
1 cup shredded coconut
3½ cups quick oatmeal
1 cup nuts
1½ cups chocolate chips

Sift first four dry ingredients together. Cream butter and sugar, add eggs and vanilla. Stir in sifted dry ingredients, coconut, oatmeal, nuts and chocolate chips. Drop by teaspoonfuls on a greased cookie sheet, bake for 15 minutes in a 350° oven.

Yield: 6 dozen

Sleeping Macaroons

4 cups quick oatmeal
2 cups brown sugar, packed
1 cup vegetable oil
2 eggs, beaten
1 tsp. salt
1 tsp. almond extract

Combine oatmeal, brown sugar and oil in bowl; blend well. Cover and let stand overnight at room temperature. The next morning, add eggs, salt and almond extract to oatmeal mixture. Blend thoroughly. Drop by teaspoonfuls on greased baking sheets. Bake in a 325° oven for 15 minutes.

Yield: 4 dozen

Scot Oat Prizes

6 oz. butterscotch chips
1 cup sugar
½ cup butter
1 egg
1 tsp. vanilla
½ tsp. almond extract
1 cup flour
½ tsp. salt
½ tsp. soda
1 cup quick oatmeal
1⅓ cups coconut

Melt butterscotch chips over hot water and set aside. Cream together sugar and butter until light and fluffy. Add egg and beat thoroughly. Blend in melted butterscotch chips, vanilla and almond extract. Sift flour, salt and soda together; stir into creamed mixture. Stir in oatmeal and coconut. Drop by rounded teaspoons on lightly greased baking sheet. Bake in a 350° oven for 12 minutes. Remove from cookie sheet immediately.

Yield: 3 dozen

Tropical Oatmeal Cookies

½ cup butter
½ cup sugar
½ cup brown sugar, packed
1 egg, beaten
1 cup crushed pineapple, *not* drained
1 cup flour
½ tsp. soda
½ tsp. salt
½ tsp. cinnamon
⅛ tsp. nutmeg
1½ cups quick oatmeal
½ cup chopped walnuts

Cream butter and sugars, beat in egg and pineapple. Sift dry ingredients together and blend into creamed mixture. Stir in oatmeal and nuts. Drop by heaping teaspoonfuls onto greased cookie sheets. Bake in a 375° oven about 15 minutes.

Yield: 3 dozen

Banana-Nut Drops

½ cup butter, softened
1 cup sugar
2 eggs
1 cup mashed ripe bananas
1 tsp. vanilla
1¾ cups flour
1½ tsp. soda
½ tsp. salt
¼ tsp. cinnamon
½ cup buttermilk
1 cup chopped nuts

Cream together butter and sugar until light and fluffy. Add eggs one at a time, beating well after each addition. Add bananas and vanilla. Sift together flour, soda, salt and cinnamon. Add dry ingredients alternately with buttermilk. Stir in nuts. Drop by teaspoonfuls, about 2 inches apart, on greased baking sheets. Bake in a 375° oven about 10 minutes.

Yield: 6 dozen

Carrot-Raisin Oat Cookies

1/3 cup brown sugar, packed
1/3 cup vegetable oil
1/3 cup molasses
1 egg
1 cup flour, *unsifted*
1/2 tsp. baking powder
1/2 tsp. soda
1/4 cup nonfat dry milk
1 tsp. salt
1/2 tsp. cinnamon
1 cup grated raw carrots
3 cups raisins
1 1/2 cups quick oatmeal

Beat together sugar, oil, molasses and egg. Sift together flour, baking powder, soda, dry milk, salt and cinnamon; blend into creamed mixture. Stir in carrots, raisins and oatmeal. Mix well. Drop by tablespoons onto greased baking sheet. Bake in a 400° oven for 10 minutes.

Yield: 3 dozen

Soft Ginger Cookies

3/4 cup butter
1 cup sugar
1/4 cup molasses
1 egg
1 3/4 cups flour
1 Tblsp. baking powder
1 tsp. cloves
1 tsp. ginger
1 tsp. cinnamon
1/2 tsp. salt

Cream butter and sugar, add molasses and egg. Sift together dry ingredients and stir into creamed mixture. Drop onto *ungreased* cookie sheet and bake in a 350° oven for 10-15 minutes.

Yield: 2 dozen

Pecan Drops

1 can sweetened condensed milk
3 oz. unsweetened chocolate
2 cups chopped pecans *or* 1 cup coconut

Melt milk and chocolate in top of double boiler, remove from heat, add pecans *or* coconut. Drop by spoonfuls on a lightly greased cookie sheet, bake 8-10 minutes in a 350° oven. Allow to cool slightly for easy removal.

Yield: 2 dozen

Drop Cream Cookies

1/2 cup butter
1 1/2 cups sugar
2 eggs
3 1/2 cups flour
1/2 tsp. soda
1/2 tsp. baking powder
1 cup sour cream
1 tsp. vanilla
cinnamon and sugar

Cream butter and sugar; beat and add eggs. Sift together dry ingredients; beat into first mixture alternately with sour cream. Add vanilla. Drop by teaspoonfuls onto a greased baking sheet, allowing 1 inch space between each cookie. Dust with sugar and cinnamon *or* sugar and chopped nutmeats *or* flaked coconut. Bake in a 350° oven for 12 minutes.

Variations: Divide batter into three parts—1 part plain, add 1/3 cup chocolate chips to another and 1/3 cup raisins to the last part.

Yield: 6 dozen

Molasses Prune Drops

¼ cup butter, softened
¼ cup brown sugar, packed
½ cup molasses
½ cup peanut butter
½ tsp. vanilla
1 egg
2 Tblsp. milk
1 cup flour
1 tsp. baking powder
½ tsp. salt
¼ tsp. soda
1 cup chopped pitted prunes

Cream together butter, brown sugar, molasses, peanut butter and vanilla until light and fluffy. Add egg and milk; creaming thoroughly. Sift together flour, baking powder, salt and soda. Stir dry ingredients into creamed mixture, blending well. Stir in prunes. Drop mixture by teaspoonfuls onto greased baking sheets. Bake in a 375° oven for 10-15 minutes.

Yield: 5 dozen

Pumpkin Cookies

½ cup butter
1 cup sugar
1 cup canned pumpkin
1 tsp. vanilla
1 tsp. soda
1 tsp. baking powder
½ tsp. cloves
1 tsp. cinnamon
½ tsp. ginger
2 cups flour
1 cup raisins
1 cup chopped nuts

Cream butter and sugar. Add pumpkin and vanilla, beat well. Sift dry ingredients together and stir into pumpkin mixture. Add raisins, nuts and stir to blend. Drop by teaspoon onto a greased cookie sheet. Bake in a 375° oven for 10 minutes.

Yield: 5 dozen

Orange Cookies

1½ cups sugar
½ cup Crisco
½ cup margarine
2 eggs
4 cups flour
½ tsp. salt
1 tsp. soda
1½ tsp. baking powder
1 cup sour cream

Cream sugar and shortenings. Add eggs and beat well. Sift together flour, salt, soda and baking powder; add alternately with sour cream. Drop by spoonfuls on a greased cookie sheet and bake in a 350° oven for 10-15 minutes. Cool.

Icing:
4 cups confectioners' sugar
1 orange, juice and grated peel
1 Tblsp. butter, melted

Combine above ingredients and frost cookies.

Yield: 6 dozen

Lemonade Drops

1 cup butter
1 cup sugar
2 eggs
3 cups flour
1 tsp. soda
6 oz. frozen lemonade concentrate, thawed
sugar

Cream together butter and sugar. Add eggs one at a time, beating well after each addition. Sift together flour and soda. Stir dry ingredients into egg mixture alternately with ½ cup of the lemonade concentrate. Drop by teaspoonfuls 2 inches apart onto *ungreased* baking sheets. Bake in upper third of 400° oven about 8 minutes, or until edges are lightly browned. Remove from oven, brush lightly with remaining concentrate, and sprinkle with sugar. Cool on racks.

Yield: 4 dozen

Frosted Apple Cookies

½ cup butter
1⅓ cups brown sugar, packed
1 egg
2 cups flour
1 tsp. soda
½ tsp. salt
1 tsp. cinnamon
½ tsp. cloves
¼ tsp. nutmeg
1 cup coarsely chopped nuts
1 cup finely chopped peeled apple
1 cup raisins
¼ cup milk
1½ cups confectioners' sugar
1 Tblsp. butter
½ tsp. vanilla
2½ Tblsp. light cream

Cream ½ cup butter and brown sugar until light and fluffy. Beat in egg and blend thoroughly. Sift together flour, soda, salt, cinnamon, cloves and nutmeg. Stir half the dry ingredients into creamed mixture. Stir in nuts, apple and raisins; then stir in remaining half of dry ingredients and milk. Mix well. Drop from tablespoon 1½ inches apart onto a lightly greased baking sheet. Bake in a 400° oven 10-12 minutes. Glaze cookies while warm. Combine confectioners' sugar, butter, vanilla and enough cream to make glaze of spreading consistency. Beat until smooth. Spread on cookies.

Yield: 4 dozen

Cranberry Cookies

½ cup butter
1 cup sugar
¾ cup brown sugar, packed
1 tsp. vanilla
⅓ cup milk
1 egg
3 cups flour
1 tsp. baking powder
¼ tsp. soda
½ tsp. salt
1 cup mixed candied fruit, diced
1 tsp. grated orange peel
2½ cups fresh cranberries, chopped

Cream together butter, sugars and vanilla. Beat in milk and egg. Sift together flour, baking powder, soda and salt. Add dry ingredients and mix well. Stir in the candied fruit, orange peel and cranberries. For each cookie use two level tablespoons of batter on a well-greased cookie sheet, about 2 inches apart. Bake in a 375° oven for 15-18 minutes.

Yield: 3½ dozen

Pineapple Cookies

½ cup butter
1 cup sugar
1 egg
2 cups flour
1 tsp. baking powder
1 tsp. soda
½ cup crushed canned pineapple, drained
sugar and nutmeg

Cream butter and sugar; add egg, beat well. Add sifted dry ingredients alternately with pineapple. Drop by teaspoonfuls onto a greased baking sheet, sprinkle with sugar and nutmeg. Bake in a 375° oven for 15 minutes.

Yield: 3 dozen

Raisin-Filled Cookies

1/4 cup raisins
1/4 cup water
2 Tblsp. sugar
1 tsp. cornstarch
1 cup butter, softened
2 cups brown sugar, packed
2 eggs
1/2 cup buttermilk
1 tsp. vanilla
3 1/2 cups flour
1 tsp. salt
1 tsp. soda
1/4 tsp. cinnamon

To prepare filling combine raisins and water, bring to a boil. Stir together sugar and cornstarch, add to raisin mixture. Set aside. Cream together butter, sugar and eggs until fluffy. Stir in milk and vanilla. Sift together flour, salt, soda and cinnamon, add to sugar mixture. For each cookie place 1 Tblsp. dough on *ungreased* cookie sheet. Place 1 Tblsp. raisin filling on dough and cover with additional 1/2 tsp. of dough. Bake in a 375° oven for 10-12 minutes.

Yield: 5-6 dozen

Chocolate-Walnut Wafers

1/2 cup butter
1 cup sugar
2 eggs, well beaten
2 oz. unsweetened chocolate, melted
1/4 tsp. vanilla
2/3 cup flour
1/4 tsp. salt
1 cup chopped walnuts

Cream butter, add sugar gradually. Add eggs, beating well. Add chocolate, vanilla and dry ingredients in order given. Drop from tip of spoon onto a greased cookie sheet 1 inch apart and bake in a 350° oven 8-10 minutes.

Yield: 3 dozen

Date-Cashew Honeys

1 1/2 cups flour, *unsifted*
1/2 tsp. baking powder
1/2 tsp. salt
1/2 cup butter
1/2 cup brown sugar, packed
1/4 cup honey
1 egg
1 tsp. vanilla
1 cup chopped pitted dates
1 1/3 cups chopped cashews

Sift together flour, baking powder and salt; set aside. Cream together butter and brown sugar in bowl until light and fluffy. Add honey, egg and vanilla, beating until well blended. Add dry ingredients into creamed mixture, mixing well. Stir in dates and cashews. Drop by teaspoonfuls on greased baking sheet. Bake in a 400° oven 10-12 minutes, or until lightly browned.

Yield: 3 1/2 dozen

Brownie Drops

2 4-oz. bars German chocolate
1 Tblsp. butter
2 eggs
3/4 cup sugar
1/4 cup flour
1/4 tsp. baking powder
1/4 tsp. cinnamon
1/2 tsp. salt
1/2 tsp. vanilla
3/4 cup finely chopped nuts

Melt chocolate and butter over hot water; set aside to cool. Beat eggs until foamy, add sugar, 2 Tblsp. at a time, beat until thick and light yellow in color. Blend in chocolate. Sift together flour, baking powder, cinnamon and salt, add to mixture and blend well. Add vanilla and chopped nuts. Drop by teaspoonfuls on a greased cookie sheet. Bake in a 350° oven for 8-10 minutes.

Yield: 2 dozen

Chocolate-Marshmallow Cookies

2 cups sifted cake flour
½ tsp. soda
½ tsp. salt
½ cup cocoa
½ cup butter
1 cup sugar
1 egg
½ cup milk
½ cup chopped pecans
1 tsp. vanilla
36 marshmallows, cut in half

Sift flour with soda, salt and cocoa; set aside. Cream butter, add sugar gradually, blending thoroughly. Add egg and beat well. Add flour mixture and milk alternately, beating after each addition. Add nuts and vanilla. Drop by teaspoonfuls 2 inches apart on a greased cookie sheet. Bake for 8 minutes in a 350° oven; top with marshmallow half cut side down. Return to oven and bake 2 minutes until marshmallow softens. Remove from pan immediately. If desired, frost cookies when cooled.

Frosting:
2½ cups confectioners' sugar
3 Tblsp. butter, softened
⅛ tsp. salt
5 Tblsp. cocoa
5 Tblsp. cream *or* milk

Combine all dry ingredients with butter. Add enough cream for smooth spreading consistency.

Yield: 6 dozen

Chocolate Fruit Drops

½ cup butter, softened
1 cup sugar
1 egg
2 oz. unsweetened chocolate, melted and cooled
¾ cup buttermilk
1 tsp. vanilla
1¾ cups flour
½ tsp. salt
½ tsp. soda
1 cup chopped pecans
1 cup cut-up dates
1 cup candied cherries

Cream butter, sugar and egg. Add cooled chocolate. Stir in buttermilk and vanilla. Sift together and stir in flour, salt and soda. Stir in nuts, dates and cherries. Chill dough. Drop dough by teaspoonfuls about 2 inches apart on an *ungreased* baking sheet. Bake in a 350° oven for 10-12 minutes. When cookies are cool, spread chocolate or white icing over tops. Garnish with cherries and nuts.

Yield: 5 dozen

Brownie Chocolate Chips

½ cup butter
1 cup sugar
2 eggs
2 oz. unsweetened chocolate, melted
1 cup flour
½ tsp. vanilla
12 oz. chocolate chips
½ cup chopped walnuts

Cream butter and sugar; add eggs, melted chocolate, flour and vanilla. Add chocolate chips and nuts. Drop by spoonfuls on a greased cookie sheet and bake in a 350° oven for 10 minutes.

Yield: 3 dozen

Chewy Chocolate Cookies

1¼ cups butter, softened
2 cups sugar
2 eggs
2 tsp. vanilla
2 cups flour, *unsifted*
¾ cup cocoa
1 tsp. soda
½ tsp. salt
12 oz. peanut butter chips

Cream butter and sugar, add eggs and vanilla, beat well. Sift together flour, cocoa, soda and salt, gradually blend into creamed mixture. Stir in chips. Drop by spoonfuls onto *ungreased* cookie sheet. Bake in a 350° oven for 8-9 minutes. (Do not overbake.) Cookies will be soft, they will puff while baking and flatten while cooling. Cool slightly and remove from cookie sheet.

Yield: 6 dozen

Chocolate-Chip Oatmeal Cookies

¾ cup sugar
¾ cup brown sugar, packed
1 cup butter
2 eggs
2 Tblsp. hot water
1½ cups flour
1 tsp. soda
1 tsp. salt
2 cups quick oatmeal
12 oz. chocolate chips
1 cup chopped nuts
1 Tblsp. vanilla

Cream together sugars and butter; beat in eggs and hot water. Sift together flour, soda and salt; add to creamed mixture. Add oatmeal, chocolate chips, nuts and vanilla. Drop by teaspoonfuls on a greased cookie sheet and bake in a 375° for 10 minutes.

Yield: 6 dozen

Chocolate-Peanut Drops

1 cup brown sugar, packed
½ cup butter, softened
1 tsp. vanilla
1 egg
1½ cups flour
¾ tsp. soda
½ tsp. baking powder
½ tsp. salt
¼ cup milk
6 oz. chocolate chips
1 cup chopped salted peanuts

Cream sugar, butter and vanilla, add egg. Sift together flour, soda, baking powder and salt; add to creamed mixture alternately with milk. Stir in chocolate chips and peanuts. Drop by tablespoonfuls onto a greased cookie sheet and bake in a 375° oven for 10-12 minutes.

Yield: 3½ dozen

White-Chocolate and Cashew Cookies

½ cup butter
1 cup brown sugar, packed
1 egg
1¾ cups flour
¼ tsp. salt
¾ tsp. soda
½ cup sour cream
2 cups white-chocolate chunks
1 cup cashew nuts

Cream butter and sugar; add egg, beat well. Sift together dry ingredients and add alternately with sour cream. Stir in chocolate and cashew nuts. Line baking sheets with aluminum foil and place large spoonfuls of batter 2 inches apart. Bake in a 375° oven for 12-14 minutes. Peel off foil and cool on racks.

Yield: 5 dozen

Chocolate Chocolate-Chip Cookies

⅔ cup flour
⅓ cup cocoa
1 tsp. baking powder
½ tsp. salt
½ cup sweet butter, softened
½ cup brown sugar, packed
½ cup sugar
1 egg
1 tsp. vanilla
6 oz. chocolate chips
½ cup pecans or walnuts

Line baking sheets with foil or parchment paper. Sift together flour, cocoa, baking powder and salt; set aside. Cream butter, add sugars and cream ingredients until blended. Add egg and vanilla; mix well. Stir in dry ingredients, chocolate chips and nuts. Drop by spoonfuls onto lightly greased cookie sheets. Bake in a 350° oven about 12 minutes, but do not overbake.

Yield: 3 dozen

Heath Bar Cookies

½ cup butter
½ cup sugar
¼ cup brown sugar, packed
1 egg
1 tsp. vanilla
1 cup + 2 Tblsp. flour
¼ tsp. soda
½ tsp. salt
1 cup Heath Bits O'Brickle

Cream butter and sugars until light and fluffy; add egg and vanilla. Sift together flour, soda and salt; add to creamed mixture. Stir in Heath candy pieces. Drop by teaspoons on a greased cookie sheet. Bake in a 375° oven for 10 minutes.

Yield: 4 dozen

Brown-Sugar Nut Cookies

1 cup butter
1 cup brown sugar, packed
½ tsp. vanilla
1 egg
1½ cups flour
½ cup chopped pecans

Cream butter and sugar until light and fluffy. Add vanilla and egg; beat well. Mix in flour and pecans. Drop small spoonfuls on greased cookie sheet 2 inches apart; they spread and flatten in baking. Bake in a 350° oven 10-12 minutes.

Yield: 3½ dozen

Sesame-Seed Cookies

1 tsp. butter
½ cup sesame seeds
¾ cup vegetable oil
1½ cups dark brown sugar, packed
2 eggs
1½ cups whole-wheat flour
½ tsp. baking powder
½ tsp. salt
½ tsp. vanilla

Melt butter in heavy frying pan over low heat. Add sesame seeds and stir until golden brown. Set aside. Cream ¾ cup oil and brown sugar until smooth, beat in eggs. Spoon flour lightly into measuring cup; sift together flour, baking powder and salt. Add to creamed mixture, mix until well blended. Stir in vanilla and toasted sesame seeds. Drop by teaspoonfuls onto lightly greased cookie sheets. Bake in a 325° oven for 8 minutes.

Yield: 5 dozen

Whole-Wheat Drop Cookies

1/4 cup butter
1/4 cup sugar
1/4 cup brown sugar, packed
1/2 tsp. grated lemon peel
1 egg, well beaten
1 cup whole-wheat flour
1 tsp. baking powder
1/8 tsp. salt
3 Tblsp. milk
1/2 cup peanuts

Cream butter, sugars and lemon peel; add well-beaten egg and beat thoroughly. Add sifted dry ingredients and milk alternately. Stir in peanuts. Drop by spoonfuls onto a greased cookie sheet. Bake in a 350° oven for about 20 minutes.

Yield: 2 dozen

Granola Cookies

1/2 cup butter, softened
1 1/4 cups brown sugar, packed
1 egg
1 1/2 cups flour
1/2 tsp. salt
1/2 tsp. soda
1/4 cup milk
2 Tblsp. wheat germ
1 1/2 cups granola
6 oz. butterscotch chips
1/2 cup raisins
1/2 cup chopped nuts

Cream butter, sugar and egg together until light and fluffy. Sift together flour, salt, soda and add alternately with milk to creamed mixture. Stir in wheat germ, granola, chips, raisins and nuts. Drop by teaspoonfuls on greased cookie sheet. Bake in a 350° oven for 8-10 minutes.

Yield: 4-5 dozen

Ice-Cream Wafers

1/2 cup butter, softened
1/2 cup sugar
1 egg
3/4 cup flour
1/4 tsp. salt
1/2 tsp. vanilla
pecan halves (about 48)

Cream butter and sugar. Add egg and beat until smooth. Add flour and salt; beat vigorously. Drop by half-teaspoonfuls well apart on a lightly greased cookie sheet, press a pecan half on each. Bake in a 350° oven about 7 minutes, until edges brown.

Yield: 4 dozen

Peanut Clusters

1/2 cup butter
1 cup brown sugar, packed
1 egg
2 cups flour
2 tsp. baking powder
1/2 cup milk
1 1/2 cups salted peanuts
8 oz. semi-sweet chocolate, melted

Cream butter and sugar together until light and fluffy. Beat in egg. Sift together flour and baking powder. Add dry ingredients to creamed mixture alternately with milk, beginning and ending with flour. Add peanuts with last addition of flour. Drop by teaspoonfuls on greased baking sheet. Bake in 350° oven for 18-20 minutes, or until lightly browned. Remove from baking sheet and cool completely. Dip one half of each cookie into melted chocolate. Place on waxed paper and chill to set chocolate.

Yield: 4 dozen

Walnut Chews

3 cups Total cereal
2 cups flour
½ tsp. soda
½ tsp. salt
¾ cup butter, softened
2 cups brown sugar, packed
2 eggs
1 cup coarsely chopped walnuts

Measure cereal, crush to 1½ cups. Set aside. Sift together flour, soda and salt; set aside. Cream butter and sugar until light and fluffy. Add eggs, beat well. Add sifted dry ingredients, nuts and crushed cereal; mix thoroughly. Drop by level tablespoonfuls onto lightly greased baking sheet about 2 inches apart. Bake in a 350° oven for about 15 minutes, or until lightly browned. Remove immediately from baking sheets, cool on wire racks.

Yield: 4½ dozen

Nutty Crisps

1 cup butter, softened
6 Tblsp. sugar
2 tsp. vanilla
2 tsp. hot water
2 cups flour
½ cup chopped walnuts or pecans
confectioners' sugar

Cream butter and sugar until light and fluffy. Add vanilla and hot water. Stir in flour and nuts. Drop by spoonfuls on a greased cookie sheet. Bake in a 350° oven for 15-20 minutes, or until edges are lightly browned. Cool 5 minutes and sift confectioners' sugar on top.

Yield: 3 dozen

JAMES ABBOTT McNEILL WHISTLER
(American, 1834–1903)
Illustration from *A Catalogue of Blue and White Nankin Porcelain*, 1878
William A. Sargent Collection

Pine-Nut Cookies

½ cup sweet butter
½ cup sugar
1 egg yolk
1 tsp. vanilla
1 cup flour
½ cup toasted pine nuts

Cream butter and sugar, beat in egg yolk and vanilla. Add flour and mix in nuts. Drop spoonfuls of batter onto a greased and floured cookie sheet. Bake in a 300° oven 20-25 minutes. While still hot, remove to rack and cool.

Yield: 2½ dozen

Very Special Oatmeal Cookies

1 egg
1 cup sugar
1 Tblsp. molasses
1 tsp. cinnamon
1 tsp. soda
2 cups flour
2½ cups quick oatmeal
½ cup chopped walnuts
½ cup raisins
1 cup melted butter

Beat the egg thoroughly. Add sugar and molasses. Sift together cinnamon, soda and flour; add to creamed mixture. Add oatmeal, walnuts and raisins. Stir in melted butter last. Drop by spoonfuls on a greased cookie sheet and press down to flatten each cookie. Bake in a 325° oven for 20 minutes.

Yield: 4 dozen

Anise Gems

1¾ cups flour
½ tsp. baking powder
½ tsp. salt
3 eggs
1 cup + 2 Tblsp. sugar
1 tsp. anise extract
2 tsp. anise seeds

Sift together flour, baking powder and salt; set aside. Beat eggs until light and lemon colored. Gradually add sugar, creaming well. Beat for 20 minutes. Blend in anise extract. Add dry ingredients to egg mixture. Sprinkle anise seeds on well-greased baking sheets. Drop dough by rounded teaspoonfuls, about 1 inch apart. Let stand overnight to dry. Bake in 325° oven for 10 minutes, or until cookies are golden color, but not browned. Any remaining anise seeds left on the baking sheets should be placed in a tightly covered tin with cookies.

Yield: 4 dozen

Peanut-Butter Crinkles

¼ cup butter
½ cup peanut butter
½ cup brown sugar, packed
½ cup sugar
1 egg
1 cup flour
½ tsp. salt
1 tsp. soda

Cream butter, peanut butter until soft. Add sugars gradually, continuing to cream until light and fluffy. Add egg; beat well. Sift flour, salt and soda together; add in two additions, beat well after each addition. Drop from teaspoon 2 inches apart, onto *ungreased* cookie sheet. Press down each cookie with a fork, press second time so that ridges are at right angles. Bake in 350° oven for 8-10 minutes.

Yield: 4½ dozen

Michigan Rocks

3 cups dates
½ cup flour
¾ cup butter
1½ cups sugar
1 Tblsp. cinnamon
½ tsp. cloves
1 Tblsp. water
2¼ cups sifted cake flour
½ tsp. salt
½ tsp. soda
4 eggs
6 cups walnuts
4 cups pecans

Cut dates in half and mix with ½ cup of flour. Cream butter and sugar, add spices and water, combine until blended. Sift together flour, salt and soda. Add eggs one at a time alternately with dry ingredients. Mix well after each addition. Add nuts, which have been coarsely chopped, and floured dates. Drop by teaspoonfuls on lightly greased cookie sheets. Bake in a 400° oven for 8 minutes.

Yield: 6-7 dozen

Crisp Spice Cookies

1½ cups butter
2 cups sugar
2 eggs
½ cup molasses
3 cups flour
1 Tblsp. soda
2 tsp. cinnamon
2 tsp. cloves
2 Tblsp. ginger

Cream butter and sugar; add eggs and molasses. Stir in dry ingredients, which have been sifted together. Drop by teaspoonfuls on greased cookie sheets about 3 inches apart. Bake in a 375° oven for 10-12 minutes.

Yield: 6 dozen

Drops of Bourbon

¼ cup butter
¾ cup sugar
2 eggs
½ cup molasses
2 cups flour
1½ tsp. soda
½ tsp. cloves
½ tsp. cinnamon
1½ Tblsp. milk
6 Tblsp. bourbon
1 cup chopped nuts
12-oz. box raisins

Cream butter and sugar, add eggs one at a time and beat well after each addition. Add molasses, dry ingredients which have been sifted together, milk and bourbon. Stir in nuts and raisins. Drop by spoonfuls on a greased cookie sheet and bake for 12 minutes in a 350° oven.

Yield: 6 dozen

Gumdrop Cookies

½ cup butter
½ cup sugar
¼ cup brown sugar, packed
1 tsp. vanilla
1 egg, beaten
1 cup + 2 Tblsp. flour
½ tsp. soda
½ tsp. salt
1 cup cut gumdrops (no licorice)
½ cup chopped walnuts

Cream butter; add sugars and cream well. Add vanilla and egg. Sift 1 cup flour, soda and salt together, add to creamed mixture. Sprinkle 2 Tblsp. flour over gumdrops. Fold dredged gumdrops into batter with nuts. Drop by teaspoonfuls, 2 inches apart on greased baking sheets. Bake in a 375° oven for 10 minutes, or until browned.

Yield: 4 dozen

Peanut-Butter Cookies

2 egg whites
1 cup sugar
1/2 tsp. vanilla
1 cup crunchy peanut butter

Beat egg whites until stiff. Beat in sugar and vanilla. Fold in peanut butter. Drop by spoonfuls onto greased cookie sheet. Bake 13-15 minutes in a 350° oven. Cool briefly before removing from cookie sheet.

Yield: 4 dozen

Peanut-Butter Options

1 can sweetened condensed milk
1/2 cup peanut butter
2 cups raisins, *OR*
2 cups Corn Flakes, crushed, *OR*
3 cups shredded coconut, *OR*
1 cup chopped nuts, *OR*
2 cups chopped dates

Combine condensed milk and peanut butter. Blend well. *Add one* of the other ingredients. Stir well. Drop by spoonfuls on a lightly greased cookie sheet. Bake in a 375° oven for 12-15 minutes. Remove at once.

Yield: 2 1/2 dozen

Melted Moments

1 cup butter
1/4 cup confectioners' sugar
1 tsp. vanilla
1/2 tsp. salt
2 cups flour

Cream butter until very light. Add sugar gradually. Add vanilla and salt. Add flour, a little at a time, beating thoroughly until fluffy. Drop from spoon onto greased cookie sheet. Bake in a 275° oven approximately 25-30 minutes. Cool and frost with butter frosting flavored with coffee.

Yield: 4 dozen

Rolled Almond Wafers

3 egg whites
3/4 cup sugar
2/3 cup flour
4 1/2 Tblsp. melted butter
2/3 cups finely chopped almonds
confectioners' sugar

Beat egg whites until stiff, add sugar a little at a time. Carefully fold in flour, melted butter and chopped almonds. Drop batter by teaspoonfuls 3 inches apart on a well-greased cookie sheet. Spread each very thin. It is best to bake only 3-4 at a time so that cookies can be shaped quickly. Bake in a 450° oven for 3-4 minutes until golden. Remove each quickly and carefully from cookie sheet with spatula and shape at once into roll with fingers. Sprinkle with confectioners' sugar. Cool on rack. Continue to bake, greasing cookie sheet each time.

Yield: 2 1/2 dozen

Lace Cookies

1 cup quick oatmeal
1 cup sugar
2 Tblsp. + 1 tsp. flour
1/4 tsp. salt
1/4 tsp. baking powder
1/2 tsp. soda
1/2 cup melted butter
1 egg, well beaten
1 1/2 tsp. vanilla

Mix dry ingredients. Pour melted butter over them. Add beaten egg and vanilla. Drop very small amounts (1/2 tsp.) on aluminum-foil-lined cookie sheet. Bake in a 325° oven about 8 minutes, until golden brown. Remove foil from pan and cool cookies. Peel carefully from foil when cooled.

Yield: 2 dozen

Chocolate Lace Cookies

1 egg, beaten
¼ cup brown sugar, packed
¼ cup sugar
1 cup old-fashioned oatmeal
½ tsp. salt
¼ tsp. almond extract
1 Tblsp. sweet butter, melted and cooled
4 oz. chocolate chips

Beat egg and sugars until mixture is thick and pale. Add oatmeal, salt, almond extract and butter; stir until well combined. Drop by teaspoonfuls 3 inches apart onto baking sheets, lined with greased foil, flatten each mound with back of fork dipped in water. Bake in the middle of a 325° oven for 7 minutes, or until golden brown. Let cookies cool on foil and gently peel away. Melt chocolate in top of double boiler. Dip each cookie into chocolate to coat half. Cool on racks.

Yield: 2 dozen

Mocha Divines

2 oz. unsweetened chocolate
2 Tblsp. butter
¼ cup flour
¼ tsp. baking powder
¼ tsp. salt
2 eggs
¾ cup sugar
2 Tblsp. instant coffee powder
1 cup chocolate chips
1 cup chopped nuts

Melt chocolate and butter. Sift together flour, baking powder and salt; set aside. Beat together eggs, sugar and coffee. Add cooled chocolate and butter to egg mixture. Stir in dry ingredients. Add chocolate chips and nuts. Line cookie sheet with foil and grease. Drop 1 inch apart. Bake for 10 minutes in a 350° oven.

Yield: 2½ dozen

MESOPOTAMIAN (Akkad), ca. 2300–2230 B.C.
Impression from a cylinder seal; steatite
Gift of Foundation for Biblical Research

Irish Lace Cookies

¾ cup brown sugar, packed
½ cup butter
2 Tblsp. flour
2 Tblsp. milk
1 tsp. vanilla
1½ cups old-fashioned oatmeal

Cream sugar and butter well. Beat in flour, milk and vanilla. Stir in oatmeal and mix well. Drop the mixture 2 inches apart on *ungreased* baking sheet. Bake in 350° oven for 10 minutes. Remove from oven and let stand for 1 minute, until firm enough to handle with spatula. Turn them over and quickly roll them into cylinders. (If they get too stiff to roll return them to the oven to soften.)

Yield: 3 dozen

Lacy Hazelnut Cookies

1¼ cups chopped hazelnuts
⅔ cup sugar
3 Tblsp. flour
1 Tblsp. cornstarch
pinch salt
3 Tblsp. butter, melted and cooled
1 tsp. vanilla
1 tsp. cinnamon
3 egg whites

Mix hazelnuts, sugar, flour, cornstarch and salt in large bowl. Blend butter, vanilla and cinnamon in small bowl. Add butter mixture to hazelnut mixture and blend well. Add egg whites and mix until smooth. Chill 30 minutes. Line baking sheet with foil. Drop batter onto prepared baking sheet by half teaspoonfuls, 2 inches apart. Dip small metal spatula into cold water. Spread cookies to width of 1¼ inches, moistening spatula for each cookie. Bake in a 400° oven until cookies are deep golden and spread 2 inches wide, about 7-8 minutes. Transfer to rack using spatula. Cool before serving. Store in airtight container.

Yield: 6 dozen

Lace Roll-Ups

1 cup flour
1 cup finely chopped nuts
½ cup light corn syrup
½ cup butter
⅔ cup brown sugar, packed

Mix flour and nuts, set aside. Heat corn syrup, butter and sugar to boiling point over medium heat, stirring constantly. Remove from heat, gradually stir in dry ingredients. Drop dough by teaspoonfuls about 3 inches apart onto a lightly greased cookie sheet. Bake only 8 or 9 cookies at one time in a 375° oven for 5 minutes, cool 3 minutes before removing. While still warm, roll into cylinders. If cookies harden, return to oven briefly. After cookies cool, fill with almond butter cream.

Filling:
2 cups confectioners' sugar
¼ cup sweet butter, softened
2 Tblsp. cream
½ tsp. almond extract

Combine all ingredients.

Yield: 4 dozen

Snappy Molasses Rolls

½ cup molasses
½ cup butter
⅔ cup sugar
1½ tsp. ginger
1 scant cup flour

Heat molasses. Add butter, then sugar. Combine with ginger and flour. Use 1 level teaspoon of dough for each snap. Drop on greased cookie sheet about 5-6 inches apart. Bake in a 350° oven for 5-6 minutes, long enough to be able to lift from cookie sheet and roll over handle of wooden spoon. If desired, the rolls may be chilled and filled with whipped cream or ice cream.

Yield: 3 dozen

Molded Cookies

Molded cookies are made from moderately stiff dough, generally workable at room temperature but sometimes chilled until firm enough to handle or of a consistency that the dough will retain the imprint of the mold. There are two types of molded cookies: shaped and pressed.

Shaped cookies are made with palms of hands or fingers to form balls or rolls, either baked as is or flattened with hand, crisscrossing with fork, or pressing with sugared glass bottom. These are baked until lightly browned and until a slight imprint remains when touched gently with finger.

Pressed cookies go through the molding plates of the cookie press. This metal cylindrical device is used for making fancy, dainty, and uniform cookies that are rich, fine-grained, and crisp. The dough should be pliable, not too warm or soft and not too cold so the dough crumbles. Pack the dough into the cookie press, making sure no air spaces are permitted. Use a *cold* cookie sheet or the shortening in the cookies will melt and pull away from the sheet when the press is lifted. Hold the press upright on an *ungreased* cookie sheet, force out the dough until it appears at the edge of the mold, release the pressure quickly, and lift the press away. Cookies are baked when set; some do not brown, others will be done when edges are lightly browned.

Apricot Balls

11-oz. box dried apricots
1 can sweetened condensed milk
2 7-oz. pkgs. flaked coconut
1 tsp. vanilla

Grind apricots, add milk, coconut and vanilla; blend well. Form balls, place on a greased cookie sheet and bake in a 325° oven for 8-10 minutes.

Yield: 2-3 dozen

Apricot Buttons

Filling:
⅓ cup dried apricots
water to cover
⅓ cup sugar

Cook apricots until water cooks down. Add sugar, mix well and cook 5 to 10 minutes over medium heat, stirring occasionally until consistency of jam. Cool.

Cookie Dough:
½ cup butter
⅓ cup sugar
1 egg yolk
½ tsp. vanilla
1 cup flour
½ tsp. salt
1 egg white
chopped nuts

Cream butter and sugar thoroughly. Stir in egg yolk and vanilla. Sift together flour and salt, mix into creamed mixture. Shape into small balls. Dip balls into unbeaten egg white; then roll in chopped nuts. Place 2 inches apart on a lightly greased baking sheet. Depress center. Bake in a 300° oven for 30 minutes. Remove from oven. While warm, fill centers with cooled apricot filling.

Yield: 3 dozen

Thimble Cookies

1½ cups butter
1 cup sugar
3 egg yolks
3 cups flour
marmalade or jam

Cream butter until soft, add sugar gradually, beat until smooth. Add egg yolks, mix well; stir in flour. Chill until firm enough to handle. Form into balls and depress center of each with thimble, fill depression with jam or marmalade of choice. If desired garnish with finely chopped nuts on top. Bake in a 350° oven for 15 minutes on a lightly greased baking sheet.

Yield: 5 dozen

Hard-Boiled-Egg Cookies

1 cup butter
½ cup sugar
2½ cups flour
3 hard-boiled egg yolks
1 tsp. vanilla
jelly

Cream butter, add sugar, mix until light and fluffy. Add flour. Put egg yolks through strainer and add with vanilla. Shape into small balls, place on lightly greased cookie sheet and depress in center. Fill center with jelly of choice. Bake in a 425° oven for 12 minutes.

Yield: 5 dozen

Whisky Crescents

1 cup butter
½ cup sugar
2½ cups flour
2 Tblsp. rye whisky
½ cup ground pecans
confectioners' sugar

Cream butter, add sugar, mix until light and fluffy. Add flour, rye and nuts. Shape into crescents, place on lightly greased baking sheet and bake in a 425° oven for 12 minutes. Sprinkle with confectioners' sugar when baked.

Yield: 5 dozen

Mexican Wedding Cakes

2 cups flour
½ cup confectioners' sugar
1 cup butter
½ cup finely ground nuts
1 Tblsp. vanilla
1 Tblsp. water
confectioners' sugar

Stir flour and confectioners' sugar together, cut in butter with pastry blender of food processor. Add nuts, vanilla and water. Form into small balls and place on greased cookie sheet. Bake in a 300° oven about 24 minutes. Roll in confectioners' sugar while warm.

Yield: 4 dozen

Christmas Cookies

1 cup butter
1½ cups sugar
2 eggs, beaten
2½ cups flour
1 tsp. soda
2 tsp. cream of tartar
½ tsp. salt
colored sugar *or* cinnamon and sugar
nut halves

Cream butter and sugar. Add eggs and blend well. Add sifted dry ingredients. Chill overnight. Form into balls, roll into colored sugar or cinnamon and sugar. Place on a greased cookie sheet and press down each with nut half in center. Bake in a 350° oven for 10 minutes.

Yield: 5 dozen

MARY CASSATT (American, 1844–1926)
Afternoon Tea Party; drypoint and aquatint in color, 1891
Gift of William Emerson and Purchase from the
Charles Henry Hayden Fund

Honey Chews

4½ cups flour
4 tsp. soda
½ tsp. salt
1½ cups butter, softened
2 cups sugar
½ cup honey
2 eggs
2 tsp. vanilla
sugar

Sift together flour, soda and salt; set aside. Cream butter and sugar until light and fluffy; blend in honey. Add eggs, one at a time, beating well after each addition. Add vanilla and dry ingredients, mix thoroughly. Shape dough into 1″ balls, arrange balls 2 inches apart on greased baking sheets. Flatten each lightly with bottom of glass dipped in sugar. Bake in 350° oven 12-15 minutes.

Yield: 7 dozen

Sensational Swedish Slims

¾ cup butter
¾ cup sugar
1 Tblsp. molasses
1½ cups flour
1½ tsp. soda

Combine all ingredients and work mixture together until well blended. Divide dough into four sections. Roll each section into a rope nearly the length of a cookie sheet. Put 2 ropes on each lightly greased cookie sheet. Press down dough with heel of hand until each rope is about 4″ to 5″ wide and 12″ long. Keep distance from each other and do not have dough too close to the edge of the pan.

Topping:
1 egg, lightly beaten
sugar
2½ oz. sliced almonds
currants (optional)

Brush each rope with beaten egg, sprinkle with sugar, and press sliced almonds into dough, and currants, if desired. Bake in a 375° oven about 10 minutes, until somewhat brown. Remove from oven, cut into 1″ strips. Cool on rack. Serve stacked like "Lincoln Logs." Store in tightly covered tin.

Yield: 4 dozen

German Pretzels

⅔ cup butter, softened
½ cup sugar
3 eggs
½ tsp. vanilla
3 cups flour
¼ tsp. salt
½ cup sugar
½ cup finely chopped nuts

Cream butter and ½ cup sugar until light and fluffy. Add 2 eggs, one at a time, beating well after each addition. Beat in vanilla. Sift together flour and salt, stir in dry ingredients, mixing well. Knead dough until smooth. Cover and let rest 1 hour at room temperature. Combine ½ cup sugar and nuts; set aside. Take a tablespoon of dough and roll on floured surface to form a slender rope. Form into a pretzel shape, or other designs like hearts or initials. Beat remaining egg slightly. Brush tops of each cookie with beaten egg and sprinkle with nut mixture. Place on *ungreased* baking sheets. Bake in a 325° oven for 25 minutes.

Yield: 3 dozen

Cinnamon Balls

1 cup butter, softened
⅓ cup sugar
2 tsp. vanilla
2 cups sifted cake flour
1 tsp. cinnamon
¾ cup Cornflake crumbs
1 cup finely chopped pecans
confectioners' sugar

Cream butter, sugar and vanilla. Sift together flour and cinnamon; add to creamed mixture. Stir in Cornflake crumbs and pecans; mix well. Shape into small balls; place on greased baking sheets. Bake for 15 minutes or longer in a 350° oven. Roll at once in confectioners' sugar.

Yield: 5 dozen

Pecan Balls

1 cup butter
½ cup sugar
2 cups sifted cake flour
1 tsp. vanilla
1 cup finely ground pecans
confectioners' sugar

Cream butter and sugar until light and fluffy. Add flour and vanilla. Mix in pecans. Roll into small balls and place on lightly greased baking sheet. Bake in a 325° oven until faintly brown, about 15 minutes. Roll while warm in confectioners' sugar.

Yield: 4 dozen

Brown-Sugar Balls

1 cup butter
½ cup brown sugar, packed
1 egg yolk
2 cups flour
1 egg white, lightly beaten
pecan *or* walnut halves

Cream butter until light and fluffy. Gradually add sugar, then egg yolk, mixing until well creamed. Add flour a little at a time. Roll into small balls and place on slightly greased cookie sheet. Dip pecan *or* walnut in egg white and press lightly onto ball flattening it a little. Bake in a 350° oven 10 to 15 minutes.

Yield: 4 dozen

Brown-Sugar Cookies

1 cup butter
2 cups brown sugar, packed
2 eggs
1 tsp. vanilla
3 cups flour
1 tsp. baking powder
⅛ tsp. salt

Cream butter and sugar, add eggs one at a time. Add vanilla. Add sifted dry ingredients and blend well. Form in teaspoon-size balls. Place 2 inches apart on a greased sheet, press flat with fork dipped in flour. Bake in a 350° oven for 8 minutes. Watch carefully; they should be lightly browned.

Yield: 6 dozen

No-Roll Sugar Cookies

1 cup sweet butter
1 cup confectioners' sugar
1 egg, beaten
1 tsp. vanilla
½ tsp. salt
2 cups flour
sugar

Cream butter and sugar until light and fluffy. Add egg, vanilla and salt. Add flour in three additions, blend well. Chill. Form into balls and place 2 inches apart on an *ungreased* cookie sheet. Moisten bottom of a glass, then dip in sugar and flatten each cookie. Bake for 15 minutes in a 375° oven.

Yield: 4 dozen

MIRIAM SCHAPIRO (American, b. 1923)
Welcome to Our Home; oil painting, 1983
Anonymous Gift

Teatime Tassies

Pastry:
3 oz. cream cheese
½ cup butter
1 cup flour

Blend together cream cheese and butter, stir in flour. Chill dough for 1 hour. Shape 2 dozen 1″ balls: place in *ungreased* 1¾-inch muffin pans. Press dough against bottoms and sides to line.

Pecan Filling:
1 egg
¾ cup brown sugar, packed
1 Tblsp. butter, softened
1 tsp. vanilla
dash of salt
1 cup broken pecans

Beat together egg, brown sugar, butter, vanilla and salt, just until smooth. Divide HALF the pecans among pastry-lined pans; add egg mixture and top with remaining pecans. Bake in a 325° oven for 25 minutes, or until filling is set. Cool and remove from pans.

Variation: Carmelized Orange Cups
Fill each pastry cup three-quarters full of orange marmalade. Bake as directed, or until marmalade has caramelized.

Yield: 2 dozen

Oatmeal Sugar Cookies

½ cup butter, softened
½ cup brown sugar, packed
½ cup sugar
1 egg
½ tsp. vanilla
½ tsp. almond extract
½ tsp. soda, dissolved in 2 tsp. vinegar
1¼ cups flour
¾ cup quick oatmeal
sugar

Cream butter and sugars until light and fluffy. Blend in egg, vanilla, almond extract, soda in vinegar. Add flour and oatmeal. Chill dough 1 hour. Roll dough to form 1″ balls, place on *ungreased* baking sheet. Flatten with bottom of glass dipped in sugar. Bake in a 350° oven for about 12 minutes.

Yield: 4 dozen

Almond Balls

1 cup sweet butter
¼ cup confectioners' sugar
2 cups flour
1 cup finely ground almonds
1 tsp. vanilla
confectioners' sugar

Cream butter with sugar until light and fluffy. Add flour, almonds and vanilla. Using a teaspoon, form dough into balls, place on a lightly greased cookie sheet and bake in a 350° oven about 15 minutes, until firm; they do not brown. Roll while warm in confectioners' sugar.

Yield: 4 dozen

Almond Cookies

½ cup almonds, ground
½ cup fine white bread crumbs
½ cup sugar
½ tsp. ginger
½ tsp. grated lemon peel
1 egg yolk

Mix together all ingredients, add egg yolk last. Let dough stand for 10 minutes. Take a tablespoon of the dough and shape it to the contours of the spoon (tends to be crumbly). Turn the spoon over and tap onto greased and floured cookie sheet. Bake for 10 minutes in a 325° oven. Let cookies cool for a minute before removing them from the pan.

Yield: 1½ dozen

Crunchy Pecan Cookies

1 cup butter, softened
1 cup brown sugar, packed
2 eggs
2 cups flour, *unsifted*
1 tsp. baking powder
¼ tsp. salt
1 tsp. vanilla
6 oz. butterscotch chips
1 cup chopped pecans
pecan halves

Cream butter and sugar, add eggs, mix well. Sift together and add flour, baking powder and salt. Stir in vanilla, butterscotch chips and chopped pecans. Shape dough into balls, press a pecan half into center of dough. Bake in a 350° oven on an *ungreased* baking sheet for 12-15 minutes.

Yield: 7 dozen

Pecan Cookies

2 cups ground pecans
⅔ cup sugar
½ tsp. salt
2 unbeaten egg whites
⅓ cup raspberry preserves
candied cherries, halved

Combine pecans, sugar and salt. Add egg whites and mix until evenly moistened. Form into small balls. Place on an *ungreased* cookie sheet. Press a small hole in the center of each ball. Fill with preserves. Top with cherry half. Bake in a 350° oven for 15 minutes. Remove from sheet at once.

Yield: 3 dozen

Chocolate-Chip Delights

1 cup butter
1 cup sugar
1 cup brown sugar, packed
2 eggs
1 tsp. vanilla
2½ cups old-fashioned oatmeal
2 cups flour
½ tsp. salt
1 tsp. baking powder
1 tsp. soda
12 oz. chocolate chips
4 oz. milk chocolate, finely grated
1½ cups chopped pecans

Cream together butter and sugars. Add eggs and vanilla, blend well. *Measure 2½ cups of oatmeal, then pulverize it in the blender.* Add oatmeal. Add flour, salt, baking powder and soda, which have been sifted together. Mix well. Add chocolate chips, grated milk chocolate and nuts. Roll into 1″ balls and place 2 inches apart on a greased cookie sheet. Bake in a 350° oven for 10-12 minutes, do not overbake. Cool 2 minutes before removing from sheet.

Yield: 5 dozen

Benne Wafers

¼ cup sesame seeds
1 Tblsp. butter, softened
½ cup brown sugar, packed
1 egg yolk
1 tsp. vanilla
½ tsp. salt
3 Tblsp. flour

Lightly brown sesame seeds in a heavy pan over moderate heat. Combine butter and brown sugar; add sesame seeds, egg yolk, vanilla and salt. Add flour and mix well. Wet hands and shape into ½″ balls. Place 2 inches apart on a lightly greased foil-lined cookie sheet. Bake on the middle rack in a 350° oven, 7-10 minutes, until firm. *Cool completely* before peeling off foil.

Yield: 3 dozen

Oatmeal Crisps

1 cup butter
2 Tblsp. water
2 Tblsp. maple syrup
1 cup flour
1 cup sugar
½ tsp. soda
1 tsp. baking powder
2½ cups quick oatmeal
½ cup sugar for rolling

Melt butter with water. Add syrup. Sift dry ingredients together and add oatmeal, mix thoroughly. Combine butter mixture with the dry ingredients and chill. Form into 1″ balls and roll in sugar. Place on *ungreased* cookie sheet and flatten slightly. Bake in a 350° oven for 12-15 minutes. Remove from sheet immediately.

Yield: 6 dozen

White-Chocolate and Macadamia-Nut Cookie

2/3 cup shredded coconut
2 1/4 cups flour, *unsifted*
1 tsp. soda
1/4 tsp. baking powder
1 tsp. salt
1 1/2 cups sweet butter
3/4 cup brown sugar, packed
3/4 cup sugar
1 egg
2 tsp. vanilla
2 cups white-chocolate chunks
1 cup salted macadamia nuts, chopped

Mix coconut and 1/4 cup flour in a food processor; set aside. Sift together remaining flour, soda, baking powder and salt. Cream butter and sugars until light and fluffy. Beat in egg and vanilla. Gradually combine coconut mixture, flour mixture into the creamed mixture. Stir in chocolate and nuts. Chill overnight. Roll into 1″ balls, place 2 inches apart on a greased cookie sheet and bake in a 350° oven for 10-12 minutes. Cool on rack.

Yield: 8 dozen

Chocolate Snowballs

3/4 cup butter
1/2 cup sugar
2 tsp. vanilla
1 egg
2 cups flour
1/2 tsp. salt
1 cup chopped nuts
6 oz. chocolate chips
confectioners' sugar

Cream butter, sugar and vanilla. Beat egg into creamed mixture. Blend in sifted dry ingredients, nuts and chocolate chips. Shape into 1″ balls. Place on *ungreased* baking sheet. Bake in a 350° oven for 15-20 minutes. Cool, then roll in confectioners' sugar.

Yield: 6 dozen

Chocolate Crinkles

1/2 cup butter
1 2/3 cups sugar
2 tsp. vanilla
2 eggs
2 oz. unsweetened chocolate, melted
2 cups flour
2 tsp. baking powder
1/2 tsp. salt
1/3 cup milk
1/2 cup chopped nuts
confectioners' sugar

Thoroughly cream together butter, sugar and vanilla. Beat in eggs, then chocolate. Sift dry ingredients together, add to creamed mixture alternately with milk, blending well after each addition. Stir in nuts. Chill 2-3 hours. Form in 1″ balls. Roll in confectioners' sugar. Place on a greased baking sheet 2-3 inches apart. Bake in a 350° oven about 15 minutes.

Yield: 4 dozen

Italian Chocolate Rum Balls

2 cups flour
2 tsp. instant coffee powder
1/8 tsp. salt
1/2 cup cocoa
2/3 cup sugar
2 cups chopped nuts
2 Tblsp. rum
1 tsp. cold water
1 1/4 cups butter
confectioners' sugar

Mix all ingredients, except confectioners' sugar, thoroughly. This can be done in food processor. Chill an hour, or overnight. Shape each tablespoon of dough into a ball. Place on lightly greased cookie sheets, about 1 inch apart. Bake in a 325° oven for 15-18 minutes. Roll while warm in confectioners' sugar, then again when cooled.

Yield: 5-6 dozen

Pfeffernuesse

1 cup + 2 Tblsp. butter
1½ cups brown sugar, packed
3 eggs
1 cup molasses
4 cups flour
1 tsp. allspice
1 tsp. cinnamon
1 tsp. cloves
1 tsp. pepper
1½ tsp. soda
1 cup chopped nuts
¼ cup citron

Cream butter and sugar, add eggs and molasses; beat well. Sift together dry ingredients. Flour nuts and citron with some of the flour. Add dry ingredients, citron and nuts and mix well. Chill dough. Roll into small balls, place on a lightly greased baking sheet and bake for 15 minutes in a 350° oven. Store in an airtight container. Mellows with age.

Yield: 7 dozen

Nutmeg Cookie Logs

3 cups flour
1 tsp. nutmeg
1 cup butter
2 tsp. vanilla
2 tsp. rum
¾ cup sugar
1 egg

Sift together flour and nutmeg; set aside. Cream butter with vanilla and rum. Gradually add sugar, creaming well. Blend in egg. Add dry ingredients. Mix thoroughly. Shape pieces of dough on lightly floured surface into long rolls, ½″ in diameter. Cut into 3″ lengths. Place on *ungreased* baking sheets. Bake in a 350° oven for 12 minutes. Cool and frost. Mark frosting with tines of fork to resemble bark. Sprinkle with nutmeg.

Frosting:
3 Tblsp. butter
½ tsp. vanilla
1 tsp. rum
2½ cups confectioners' sugar
2-3 Tblsp. cream

Cream butter, vanilla and rum. Add sugar alternately with 2-3 Tblsp. of cream, beating until spreading consistency.

Yield: 4 dozen

Stuffed Monkeys

¼ cup butter
½ cup sugar
1 egg, beaten
1 cup flour
1 tsp. baking powder
¼ tsp. salt
1 cup chopped dates
1 cup chopped walnuts
sugar

Cream butter and sugar until light and fluffy. Add egg. Sift together flour, baking powder and salt, blend well with creamed mixture. Stir in dates and walnuts. Shape into small balls, roll in sugar, place on a greased cookie sheet and bake in a 375° oven for 10 minutes.

Yield: 3 dozen

Velvet Spritz Cookies

1 cup butter
⅔ cup sugar
2 egg yolks, beaten
2½ cups sifted cake flour
1 tsp. almond extract

Cream butter, add sugar, beat thoroughly. Add beaten egg yolks, flour and extract. Fill cookie press, force dough through press in shapes onto an *ungreased* cookie sheet. Bake in a 375° oven for 8-12 minutes.

Yield: 5 dozen

SUZUKI HARUNOBU (Japanese, 1725–1770)
Ofuji Visits Osen at the Hagiya Teashop; woodblock print
Spaulding Collection

Raisin Ginger Cookie

¾ cup butter
1 cup sugar
1 egg
¼ cup molasses
2¼ cups flour
1 tsp. salt
2 tsp. soda
¼ tsp. cloves
1 tsp. ginger
½ tsp. cinnamon
1½ cups raisins
sugar

Cream butter and sugar, add egg. Add molasses, continue creaming until well blended. Sift together flour, salt, soda and spices; add to creamed mixture. Blend well. Stir in raisins. Chill dough until firm enough to handle. Shape into small balls and roll in additional sugar. Place on a lightly greased baking sheet and bake in a 375° oven for 8-10 minutes.

Yield: 3 dozen

Friendship Gingersnaps

¾ cup butter
1 cup sugar
¼ cup molasses
1 egg, beaten
2 cups flour
¼ tsp. salt
2 tsp. soda
1 tsp. cinnamon
1 tsp. ginger
sugar

Cream butter and sugar. Beat in molasses and egg. Add sifted dry ingredients and beat well. Chill. Form into small balls, roll in sugar and place on a greased baking sheet. Bake in a 325° oven for 15 minutes.

Yield: 5 dozen

Ginger Rounds

1 cup flour
1 tsp. soda
¼ tsp. salt
½ tsp. cinnamon
1 tsp. ginger
¼ tsp. cloves
¼ tsp. allspice
⅛ tsp. black pepper
6 Tblsp. butter
½ cup brown sugar, packed
1 egg
2 Tblsp. molasses
1 Tblsp. grated lemon peel
1 Tblsp. grated orange peel
sugar

Sift together flour, soda and spices; set aside. Cream together butter and sugar, add egg and molasses, continue creaming. Add grated peels and dry ingredients. Chill dough for 4 hours. Sprinkle sugar into plate, pinch pieces of dough, ½″ in size, roll in sugar and place on well-greased cookie sheet. Bake in a 350° oven for 10 minutes.

Yield: 5 dozen

Sherry Tumblers

1 cup butter
2 cups sugar
3 eggs
1 tsp. vanilla
3 Tblsp. sherry
3 cups flour

Cream butter, add sugar gradually while continuing to cream, beat until light and fluffy. Add eggs, mix well. Add vanilla and sherry. Add flour a little at a time, mixing well after each addition. Chill dough until firm; fill cookie press, force dough through press onto a lightly greased cookie sheet, bake in a 400° oven for 15 minutes.

Yield: 8 dozen

Butterscotch Pressed Cookies

¾ cup butter
1 cup brown sugar, packed
1 egg, beaten
½ tsp. vanilla
2 cups flour
1 tsp. baking powder

Cream butter and sugar. Add beaten egg and vanilla, mix well. Add flour and baking powder sifted together. Mix thoroughly and pack firmly into the cookie press. Force dough through press in desired shapes and onto an *ungreased* cookie sheet. Bake in a 400° oven for 8-12 minutes.

Yield: 5 dozen

Rich Chocolate Teas

½ cup butter
1 cup sugar
1 egg, beaten
½ tsp. vanilla
½ tsp. salt
2 Tblsp. milk
2 cups sifted cake flour
2 oz. unsweetened chocolate, melted

Cream butter, add sugar gradually, cream well. Add beaten egg, vanilla, salt and milk. Blend and add half the sifted flour. When well mixed, add melted chocolate and remainder of the flour. Mold with cookie press on cold, *ungreased* cookie sheet. Bake in a 325° oven for 23 minutes.

Yield: 6 dozen

Peanut-Butter Spritz

1¾ cups flour
¼ tsp. salt
¾ cup butter, softened
3 Tblsp. creamy peanut butter
½ cup sugar
1 egg yolk
½ tsp. vanilla

Sift together flour and salt; set aside. Cream together butter, peanut butter and sugar until light and fluffy. Add egg yolk and vanilla, creaming well. Add dry ingredients, stirring until thoroughly blended. Force dough through cookie press 1 inch apart on *ungreased* baking sheets. Bake in a 375° oven for 6-8 minutes.

Yield: 5 dozen

Pineapple Pressed Cookies

4½ cups flour
1 tsp. baking powder
⅛ tsp. salt
1½ cups bufter, softened
1 cup sugar
1 egg
2 Tblsp. thawed frozen pineapple juice concentrate

Sift together flour, baking powder and salt; set aside. Cream together butter and sugar until light and fluffy. Beat in egg and pineapple juice concentrate. Add dry ingredients, mixing well. Force dough through cookie press 1 inch apart, on *ungreased* baking sheet. Bake in a 375° oven 8-10 minutes.

Yield: 8-9 dozen

No-Bake Cookies

As the name suggests, No-Bake Cookies do not have a baked dough. Ingredients like fruits, nuts, and grains are combined with melted chocolate, melted butter, or liquids to moisten mixture into a manageable union. Cookies are pressed into a pan to be sliced or formed into drops, balls, or logs. Often the shaped cookies are chilled to set until firm so that ingredients adhere to each other. Cookies should have a favorable texture and please the eye as well as the palate.

Date Cookies

1 cup sugar
½ cup butter
2½ cups chopped dates
1 egg
2 cups chopped pecans
2 cups Rice Krispies
pinch salt
1 tsp. vanilla
shredded coconut

Cook sugar, butter and dates over medium heat for 15 minutes, remove from heat and add egg. Cool. Add nuts, Rice Krispies, salt and vanilla. Form into balls and roll in shredded coconut. Chill.

Yield: 6 dozen

Date Balls

2 cups bran flakes
¾ cup pitted dates
½ cup pecans
2 Tblsp. honey
1 Tblsp. butter, softened
2 Tblsp. lemon juice
confectioners' sugar

Put cereal, dates and nuts in food processor. Add honey, butter and lemon juice. Knead mixture until well blended. Shape into 1″ balls or fingers, and roll in confectioners' sugar. Decorate with pecan halves. If desired, omit confectioners' sugar and dip in melted chocolate.

Yield: 3 dozen

Date Crisps

3 cups dates, chopped
1 or 2 Tblsp. water
2 cups sugar
4 eggs, well beaten
½ tsp. salt
5 cups Rice Krispies
chopped nuts or shredded coconut

Place dates, water, sugar, eggs and salt in saucepan; blend. Cook until mixture leaves the sides of the pan. Add Rice Krispies. Cool. Roll in small balls and cover with chopped nuts or shreddded coconut.

Yield: 6 dozen

Fruit-Pecan Balls

½ cup dried apricots, coarsely chopped
½ cup prunes, coarsely chopped
¼ cups raisins, minced
3 Tblsp. Cointreau
¾ tsp. grated orange peel
¾ cup sweetened flaked coconut
¾ cup pecans, toasted and chopped fine
¾ cup sugar

Combine apricots, prunes, raisins, Cointreau and orange peel, macerate for 1 hour, chop fine in a processor. Stir together coconut, pecans and fruit mixture until the mixture holds together, shape rounded teaspoons of the mixture into balls. Roll the balls in sugar and store them in an airtight container.

Yield: 3 dozen

JAPANESE, late 17th or early 18th century
Teapot with flowers; porcelain with overglaze enamel decoration (Kakiemon ware)
Keith McLeod Fund

Chocolate Fruit Bars

½ cup pine nuts *or* almonds
½ cup pitted dates
½ cup raisins
½ cup citron peel
½ cup candied lemon peel
¼ cup currants
1 egg white
2 Tblsp. water
1 tsp. vanilla
confectioners' sugar
6 oz. chocolate chips, melted

Chop nuts and fruits in food processor. Place egg white in a bowl, beat lightly, blend with water and vanilla. Add nuts, fruits and enough sifted confectioners' sugar to form a stiff paste. Pat into 8x8x2-inch lightly greased pan lined with waxed paper. Let mixture dry for 4 hours. Spread half the melted chocolate over bars. When set, turn out on waxed paper and spread the other side with the balance of the chocolate.

Yield: 2½ dozen

Chocolate Rum Drops

1 cup almond paste
1 cup confectioners' sugar
8 oz. unsweetened chocolate, grated
3 Tblsp. rum
1 Tblsp. butter
1½ Tblsp. cinnamon
½ cup cocoa

Mix almond paste with sugar, chocolate, rum and butter. When well blended, form into balls and roll in a mixture of cocoa and cinnamon. Chill.

Yield: 5 dozen

Honey Rum Balls

2 cups vanilla wafer crumbs
½ cup rum
½ cup honey
1 lb. shelled walnuts, ground
confectioners' sugar

Mix vanilla wafer crumbs, rum, honey and ground walnuts. Shape into small balls and roll in confectioners' sugar. Store in an air-tight container. Dust again with sugar before serving.

Yield: 5 dozen

Orange Balls

2 cups vanilla wafer crumbs
¾ cup flaked coconut
¾ cup confectioners' sugar
½ cup frozen orange juice concentrate
confectioners' sugar

Combine vanilla wafer crumbs, coconut and confectioners' sugar. Add orange juice concentrate. Make 1″ balls. Roll in confectioners' sugar. Freeze. Defrost to serve.

Yield: 2 dozen

Chocolate Marshmallow Haystacks

3 oz. cream cheese
2 Tblsp. milk
2 cups sugar
2 oz. unsweetened chocolate, melted
¼ tsp. vanilla
dash salt
2 cups miniature marshmallows
flaked coconut

Combine softened cream cheese and milk, mixing until well blended. Gradually add sugar. Stir in chocolate, vanilla and salt; fold in marshmallows. Drop rounded teaspoons of the mixture in coconut; toss until well covered. Place on baking sheet. Chill until firm.

Yield: 4 dozen

Cathedral Cookies

12 oz. chocolate chips
¼ cup butter
2 eggs
2 cups confectioners' sugar
1 tsp. vanilla
10½-oz. pkg. small colored marshmallows
1½ cups chopped nuts
24 graham crackers, crushed

Melt chocolate chips and butter together. Beat eggs and confectioners' sugar, add vanilla and chocolate mixture; mix well. Fold in marshmallows and nuts. Divide into six parts. Place graham cracker crumbs on waxed paper. Moisten hands and shape each part into logs 2″ in diameter, then roll in crumbs. Roll in waxed paper and chill. Slice ¼″ thick.

Yield: 4 dozen

No-Bake Chocolate Cookies

2 cups sugar
½ cup milk
½ cup cocoa
½ cup butter
½ cup crunchy peanut butter
1 tsp. vanilla
3 cups quick oatmeal
½ cup coconut (optional)

Mix sugar, milk, cocoa and butter together and boil for 1 minute, remove from heat. Add peanut butter and vanilla. After peanut butter has melted pour over oatmeal and coconut. Stir well and drop by teaspoonfuls on waxed-paper-lined cookie sheet. Let stand for 1 hour. Store in refrigerator in a tight container. Keeps well.

Yield: 5 dozen

Whisky Balls

3 cups vanilla wafer crumbs
½ cup finely chopped pecans
½ cup cocoa
2 cups confectioners' sugar
½ cup whisky
3 Tblsp. light corn syrup
dash salt

Prepare vanilla wafer crumbs in a food processor. Chop the nuts in the processor and blend together with crumbs, cocoa, 1 cup confectioners' sugar, whisky, corn syrup and dash salt. Form into small balls, about walnut size. Roll each ball in the remaining cup of confectioners' sugar. Place on a cookie sheet. Chill in the refrigerator overnight.

Yield: 3 dozen

No-Cook Rum Drops

2 cups finely crushed graham cracker crumbs, sifted
2 Tblsp. cocoa
1 cup confectioners' sugar
⅛ tsp. salt
1 cup chopped nuts
1½ Tblsp. honey
¼ cup rum

Mix graham cracker crumbs, cocoa, sugar, salt and nuts. In a separate bowl, combine honey and rum. Gradually stir honey into dry ingredients, until mixture holds together. Add more rum if it is too dry. Form into 1" balls and roll in confectioners' sugar. Age in a cookie tin for at least a day.

Yield: 5 dozen

No-Bake Bars

½ cup sugar
½ cup light corn syrup
¾ cup peanut butter
½ tsp. vanilla
3 cups Special K cereal
12 oz. chocolate chips

Mix sugar and corn syrup, bring to a boil. Remove from heat and add peanut butter, vanilla and cereal. Spread on a greased 15x10-inch jelly-roll pan and pat out evenly. Melt chocolate and spread over the top. Refrigerator for one hour or more. Break into bite sized pieces.

Yield: 5 dozen

Nut Fudge Bars

1 cup butter
2 cups confectioners' sugar
2 egg yolks
1 tsp. vanilla
8 oz. sweet chocolate, melted
1 cup chopped walnuts
2 egg whites, stiffly beaten
20 chocolate-chip cookies, finely rolled

Cream butter and sugar together. Add egg yolks and beat until light and fluffy. Add vanilla and melted chocolate, blend well. Stir in chopped nuts; fold in beaten egg whites. Line a 11x7x2-inch pan with waxed paper, sprinkle with 1/2 cookie crumbs over bottom of pan, spread mixture evenly over crumbs, sprinkle remaining crumbs over top, press firmly onto chocolate mixture. Chill for three hours.

Yield: 3 1/2 dozen

Mint Squares

1 1/4 cups butter
1/2 cup cocoa
3 1/2 cups confectioners' sugar
1 egg, beaten
1 tsp. vanilla
2 cups graham cracker crumbs
1/3 cup green creme de menthe
1 1/2 cups chocolate chips

Bottom Layer:
Combine 1/2 cup butter and cocoa. Heat and stir until well blended. Remove from heat and add 1/2 cup sifted confectioners' sugar, egg and vanilla. Stir in graham cracker crumbs, mix well and press into *ungreased* 15x10-inch jelly-roll pan. Press firmly, spread evenly and thinly.

Middle Layer:
Melt 1/2 cup butter. Combine butter, creme de menthe and 3 cups sifted confectioners' sugar; mix until smooth. Spread over bottom layer and chill one hour.

Top Layer:
Combine 1/4 cup butter and chocolate chips in double boiler until well mixed. Spread over mint layer. Chill 1-2 hours. Cut in small squares and store in refrigerator.

If desired, substitute 1/3 cup cream, 1 tsp. peppermint extract and green food coloring for creme de menthe.

Yield: 5 dozen

Three-Layer Chocolate Squares

Crust:
1/2 cup butter
1/4 cup cocoa
1/2 cup confectioners' sugar
1 egg, slightly beaten
2 tsp. vanilla
3 cups graham cracker crumbs
1/2 cup chopped pecans

Melt butter. Add all the ingredients, one at a time stirring after each addition until mixture is well blended. Press into 13x9x2-inch pan.

Filling:
1/4 cup butter
1 tsp. cornstarch
2 tsp. sugar
3 Tblsp. light cream
1 tsp. vanilla
2 cups confectioners' sugar
9 3/4-oz. sweet-chocolate bar

Melt butter. Combine cornstarch and sugar. Add to butter and blend thoroughly. Add cream. Cook, stirring constantly, until thick and smooth. Cool. Add vanilla and confectioners' sugar. Blend well and spread over first layer. This is a stiff mixture; drop by teaspoonfuls and spread carefully. Melt chocolate bar over hot water. Spread over second layer. Cool at room temperature and cut into 1″ squares before chocolate is firm.

Yield: 10 dozen

Fudge Balls

8-oz. pkg. chocolate wafers, crushed, *or* 1½ cups crumbs
16-oz. can chocolate frosting
1-2 Tblsp. coffee *or* orange liqueur
cocoa or coconut or chopped nuts or chocolate jimmies

Combine cookie or cake crumbs with frosting. Moisten with liqueur to achieve workable consistency. Form into dainty balls, about ¾″ in diameter. Roll in sifted cocoa *or* grated coconut *or* finely chopped nuts *or* chocolate jimmies. Store in refrigerator.

Yield: 3-4 dozen

Mocha Rolls

1 cup vanilla wafer crumbs
¼ cup chopped pecans
¼ cup confectioners' sugar
½ tsp. cocoa
1 tsp. instant coffee powder
1 tsp. light corn syrup
2 Tblsp. water
confectioners' sugar

Roll or process vanilla wafers into fine crumbs and measure. Combine crumbs, pecans, sugar, cocoa and coffee. Add syrup and water. For each roll, measure level tablespoon and shape into roll 1½″ long. Roll in extra confectioners' sugar.

Yield: 1½ dozen

Ginger Balls

4 cups confectioners' sugar
½ cup butter, softened
1 egg
pinch salt
1⅓ cup crystallized ginger, cut fine
½ cup nuts, finely chopped
vanilla wafers, crushed

Combine above ingredients except for vanilla crumbs and chill until firm. Form into balls about 1″ in diameter; roll balls in finely ground vanilla-wafer crumbs. Refrigerate or freeze.

Can be made by chopping ginger and nuts in food processor and adding remaining ingredients.

Yield: 5 dozen

Coconut-Sesame Clusters

6 oz. chocolate chips
⅓ cup seasame seeds, toasted
1 cup sweetened flaked coconut plus additional for sprinkling on the clusters

Melt chocolate chips in a double boiler. Remove from heat; add sesame seeds and 1 cup coconut; combine mixture well. Drop rounded teaspoons of the mixture onto a waxed-paper-lined baking sheet. Sprinkle with additional coconut. Chill until hardened and store in an airtight container.

Yield: 2 dozen

Date-Sesame Cookies

2½ oz. sesame seeds
8 oz. chopped dates
1 cup sugar
½ cup butter, melted
1 egg, beaten
2 cups Rice Krispies
½ cup chopped walnuts

Lightly toast sesame seeds in 300° oven. Combine dates, sugar, butter and egg in saucepan and mix well, cook over low heat for 7 minutes, stirring constantly. Remove from heat, add Rice Krispies and nuts. Drop teaspoonfuls onto waxed paper to cool. Roll in toasted sesame seeds.

Yield: 4 dozen

JEAN SIMEON CHARDIN (French, 1699–1779)
Still Life with Teapot, Grapes, Chestnuts, and a Pear;
oil painting, 1764
Gift of Martin Brimmer

Refrigerator Cookies

Refrigerator cookies are made from a rich dough. Stiff dough may be inclined to crumble; soft dough must be chilled before forming into rolls. Form into smooth compact rolls and wrap tightly in waxed paper or form into a pan mold.

Thoroughly chill dough for several hours or overnight. Unbaked dough can be stored for one week in refrigerator or for six months in the freezer. When ready to bake, cut uniform slices as the recipe recommends. Cut with a sharp, thin knife in a sawing motion, using as little pressure as possible. Do not press too hard, or allow dough to become softened. Keep knife wiped clean. Place cookies 2 inches apart on baking sheet to allow for spreading.

Refrigerator cookies are generally thin and crisp, well flavored, tender, and lightly browned.

Javanese Shortbread

1 cup sweet butter, softened
¾ cup sugar
1 cup flaked coconut
2 cups flour

Cream softened butter and sugar thoroughly, add coconut and flour, mix only until blended. Chill until stiff enough to handle and form into half-dollar-sized rolls using waxed paper to wrap. Refrigerate until firm. Cut in ¼″ slices. Bake on *ungreased* cookie sheets in a 300° oven for 20-30 minutes. Do not brown; they should be golden brown on the bottom. Cool for 2 minutes before removing from cookie sheets. Dust generously with confectioners' sugar. Store in airtight container.

Yield: 5 dozen

Pecan Shortbread

1 cup butter
⅔ cup confectioners' sugar
1½ cups flour
1 cup finely chopped pecans, lightly toasted
⅛ tsp. salt

Cream butter with sugar. Stir in flour, pecans and salt. Chill until firm enough to handle. Form into two 7″ rolls and wrap in waxed paper. Chill overnight. Slice into ¼″ slices, arrange 2 inches apart on an *ungreased* baking sheet and bake for 12-15 minutes in a 375° oven, until edges are golden.

Yield: 5 dozen

Coconut Cookies

5½ cups flour
3 tsp. baking powder
¼ tsp. salt
1½ cups melted butter
1 cup sugar
½ cup brown sugar, packed
3 eggs, slightly beaten
4 cups shredded coconut, chopped

Sift together flour, baking powder and salt; set aside. Melt butter and cream with sugars. Add beaten eggs. Stir in flour mixture and coconut; mix well. Pack into an 8x8x2-inch pan lined with waxed paper. Chill thoroughly. Remove from pan, cut into four 2″ bars, slice in ⅛″ slices. Bake on *ungreased* baking sheet for 5-10 minutes in a 400° oven.

Yield: 7 dozen

Almond Slices

2¼ cups flour
1 tsp. salt
1 tsp. soda
1 cup butter
1 cup brown sugar, packed
1 tsp. almond extract
2 eggs, beaten
1 egg, lightly beaten
1 Tblsp. water
30 whole blanched almonds

Sift together flour, salt and soda; set aside. Cream butter, sugar and almond extract about 5 minutes. Add 2 beaten eggs; stir in dry ingredients and mix until dough forms a smooth ball. Transfer dough onto a lightly floured surface. Divide the dough into two equal portions and form two rolls. Wrap in waxed paper and chill thoroughly. Cut each roll into 15 slices. Lay each onto a greased cookie sheet. Slightly flatten the edge of each round with your hand. Gently press an almond in the center of each cookie. Mix egg with water and lightly brush the cookies with the glaze. Bake for 10-12 minutes until puffed and golden brown in a 350° oven. Cool.

Yield: 2½ dozen

Dollar Cookies

1 cup butter
1 cup margarine
1 tsp. vanilla
1 cup sugar
4 cups flour
½ tsp. salt

Cream butter and margarine together, add vanilla, gradually add sugar, flour and salt; mix to a dough. Divide dough in four parts, form rolls and wrap in waxed paper. Chill in refrigerator overnight. Slice ¼″ thick and bake on an *ungreased* cookie sheet for 10-15 minutes in a 350° oven.

Yield: 8 dozen

Butterscotch Nut Cookies

½ cup melted butter
1 cup brown sugar, packed
1 egg
1 tsp. vanilla
½ cup nuts
1¾ cups flour
½ tsp. salt
½ tsp. soda

Melt butter and combine with sugar. Add egg, vanilla and nuts. Sift together dry ingredients and stir into above mixture. Line an 8x8x2-inch pan with waxed paper, pat down mixture in pan, chill overnight. Remove from pan, cut into four 2″ bars, and slice cookies thin. Place on an *ungreased* baking sheet. Bake for 8-10 minutes in a 350° oven.

Yield: 7 dozen

Lemon Tangs

¾ cup sweet butter, softened
1 cup sugar
1 tsp. vanilla
1½ Tblsp. grated lemon peel
¼ cup fresh lemon juice
2¼ cups flour
1½ tsp. baking powder
½ tsp. soda
¼ tsp. salt
confectioners' sugar

Cream butter and sugar until light and fluffy. Add vanilla, lemon peel and juice, beat until smooth. Sift together dry ingredients, add to creamed mixture and blend well. Chill dough for 1 hour. Using waxed paper, form dough into rolls 1½″ in diameter. Chill rolls overnight. Cut into slices ⅛″ thick. Bake on an *ungreased* cookie sheet in a 350° oven for about 8 minutes, or until edges are golden brown. Cool on racks and sprinkle tops with confectioners' sugar.

Yield: 4 dozen

Anise Wafers

2½ cups flour
½ tsp. salt
1 cup butter, softened
3 oz. cream cheese, softened
1 cup sugar
1 egg yolk
½ tsp. vanilla
2 tsp. anise seeds

Sift together flour and salt; set aside. Cream together butter, cream cheese and sugar until light and fluffy. Add egg yolk, vanilla and anise seeds; beat well. Stir in dry ingredients; blend well. Shape dough into two rolls and wrap in waxed paper. Chill for four hours. Cut ⅛″ slices and bake on *ungreased* baking sheets in a 350° oven for 10-12 minutes.

Yield: 6 dozen

Cinnamon Rounds

1 cup chopped almonds
2 cups flour
1 tsp. cinnamon
½ tsp. salt
1 cup butter, softened
1 cup sugar
1 egg

Spread almonds in 13x9x2-inch pan and toast in a 350° oven 15 minutes, stirring 2 or 3 times. Cool completely. Sift together flour, cinnamon and salt; set aside. Cream together butter and sugar until light and fluffy. Add egg and beat well. Stir in dry ingredients, mix thoroughly. Add toasted almonds. Shape dough into two 7″ rolls. Wrap rolls in waxed paper and chill for four hours. Cut ¼″ slices and place on greased baking sheets. Bake in a 350° oven until golden brown about 8 minutes.

Yield: 4 dozen

Spice Cookies

½ cup butter
½ cup molasses
1 egg, beaten
2½ cups flour
¼ tsp. salt
½ tsp. soda
½ tsp. baking powder
¼ tsp. ginger
¼ tsp. cinnamon
¼ tsp. allspice

Cream butter until light, add molasses and beaten egg; beat thoroughly. Sift all dry ingredients together and add gradually to first mixture. Form into rolls, wrap in waxed paper and chill overnight. Cut in very thin slices and place on a lightly greased cookie sheet. Bake in 375° oven for 5-7 minutes, only until set. Overbaking will cause a bitter taste to cookies made without sugar.

Yield: 6 dozen

Chocolate Spice Rounds

½ cup butter, softened
⅔ cup sugar
1 egg, lightly beaten
3 oz. unsweetened chocolate, melted
1¼ cups flour
1 tsp. baking powder
½ tsp. cinnamon
⅛ tsp. *each* cloves, salt, allspice, nutmeg and pepper

Cream butter and sugar, add egg and melted chocolate. Sift together dry ingredients and stir into chocolate mixture. Chill dough until firm enough to handle. Form into two 6″ rolls and wrap in waxed paper. Chill overnight. Cut into ¼″ slices and arrange 2 inches apart on lightly greased baking sheets. Bake for 10 minutes in a 375° oven.

Yield: 4 dozen

WALTER CRANE (British, 1845–1915)
Polly Put the Kettle On; color wood engraving
from *The Baby's Bouquet*
Gift of Ellen T. Bullard

Wheat Thins

1½ cups quick oatmeal
¾ cup whole-wheat flour
¼ cup wheat germ
½ tsp. soda
¼ tsp. salt
½ cup butter, softened
½ cup sugar
½ cup brown sugar, packed
1 egg
1 tsp. vanilla
¾ cup dry-roasted sunflower seeds

Mix together oatmeal, whole wheat flour, wheat germ, soda and salt; set aside. Cream together butter and sugars until light and fluffy. Add egg and vanilla; beat well. Add dry ingredients mixing well. Stir in sunflower seeds. Divide dough in half and form two rolls. Wrap in waxed paper and chill in refrigerator four hours. Cut ¼″ slices and place slices on *ungreased* baking sheets about 2 inches apart. Bake in a 375° oven 10-12 minutes, or until lightly browned.

Yield: 4 dozen

Cardamom Thins

¾ cup butter, softened
⅔ cup brown sugar, packed
¼ cup light cream
1½ cups flour
2 tsp. cardamom
½ tsp. soda
½ tsp. salt

Cream together butter and sugar, beat in light cream. Sift together dry ingredients and add to creamed mixture. Chill dough until firm enough to handle. Form into a 10″ roll, wrap in waxed paper and chill overnight. Cut in ¼″ slices and arrange on an *ungreased* baking sheet 2 inches apart. Bake in a 375° oven for 6-8 minutes.

Yield: 3½ dozen

Caraway Crisps

¾ cup butter, softened
½ cup brown sugar, packed
½ cup sugar
⅓ cup sour cream
1 tsp. grated lemon peel
2 cups flour
½ tsp. soda
¼ tsp. salt
2 tsp. caraway seeds

Cream butter and sugars together. Beat in sour cream and lemon peel. Sift together dry ingredients and add to creamed mixture. Add caraway seeds. Chill dough until firm enough to handle. Form into a 12″ roll, chill 4 hours. Cut into ¼″ slices and arrange 2 inches apart on an *ungreased* baking sheet; bake in a 375° oven for 6-8 minutes.

Yield: 4 dozen

Icebox Oatmeal Cookies

1 cup butter
1 cup sugar
1 cup brown sugar, packed
2 eggs, beaten
1 tsp. vanilla
1½ cups flour
1 tsp. salt
1 tsp. soda
3 cups quick oatmeal
½ cup chopped nuts

Cream together butter and sugars until light and fluffy. Add beaten eggs and vanilla. Sift together flour, salt and soda; add to creamed mixture. Blend well. Add oatmeal and nuts. Shape in rolls 1½″ in diameter, wrap in waxed paper and chill overnight in refrigerator. Slice ¼″ thick. Bake on an *ungreased* cookie sheet for 10 minutes in a 350° oven.

Yield: 6 dozen

Bran Refrigerator Snaps

½ cup butter
½ cup sugar
½ cup molasses
½ cup all-bran
2 cups flour
¼ tsp. salt
1½ tsp. soda
1½ tsp. cinnamon
1½ tsp. ginger

Thoroughly cream butter, sugar and molasses. Add all-bran and sifted dry ingredients; mix thoroughly. Shape in roll, about 1½″ in diameter; chill. Slice thin. Arrange on greased cookie sheet. Bake in a 375° oven for 10 minutes.

Yield: 4 dozen

Date Pinwheels

8-oz. pkg. pitted dates
¼ cup sugar
dash of salt
½ cup water
1 cup chopped nuts
½ cup butter
½ cup brown sugar, packed
½ cup sugar
1 egg
½ tsp. vanilla
2 cups flour
¼ tsp. soda
¼ tsp. salt

Cut dates in small pieces, add ¼ cup sugar, dash of salt and ½ cup water. Simmer for 5 minutes. Remove from heat. Add nuts. Cool. Cream butter and sugars; add egg and vanilla. Beat until light. Sift together flour, soda and salt; add and blend. Roll dough into two parts on floured waxed paper and spread each with date filling. Roll and wrap in waxed paper and chill overnight. Slice thin and place on a greased baking sheet. Bake for 10 minutes in a 375° oven.

Yield: 6 dozen

Pinwheels

½ cup butter
½ cup sugar
1 egg yolk
1 tsp. vanilla
1½ cups flour
⅛ tsp. salt
1½ tsp. baking powder
3 Tblsp. milk
1 oz. unsweetened chocolate, melted

Cream butter and add sugar gradually, add egg yolk and vanilla; beat well. Add sifted dry ingredients and milk alternately. Divide dough in half, add the melted chocolate to one half of the mixture. Roll the chocolate half of the dough into a rectangle 4x6″ and ¼″ thick. Roll the white half of the dough into a rectangle 4x6″ and ¼″ thick. Place white rectangle on the chocolate and roll as for a jelly roll. Chill overnight, slice ⅛″ thick and bake in a 375° oven for 5-10 minutes.

Yield: 3 dozen

Chocolate Cookies

2 cups flour
½ tsp. baking powder
1 tsp. cinnamon
¼ tsp. salt
½ cup butter, softened
⅔ cup sugar
1 egg
¼ cup chocolate syrup
¾ cup chopped nuts

Sift together flour, baking powder, cinnamon and salt; set aside. Cream butter and sugar until light and fluffy. Beat in egg and chocolate syrup. Stir in flour mixture. Shape into roll 2″ in diameter. Roll in the nuts. Wrap in waxed paper, chill overnight. Cut ⅜″ slices. Place 1 inch apart on a greased cookie sheet. Bake in a 350° oven for 15 minutes. Cool on rack.

Yield: 3 dozen

Peanut-Butter Refrigerator Cookies

1¾ cups flour
½ tsp. soda
½ tsp. salt
½ cup peanut butter
¼ cup butter, softened
1 cup brown sugar, packed
1 egg
¼ cup evaporated milk

Sift together flour, soda and salt; set aside. Cream together peanut butter and butter; add brown sugar gradually and beat until light and fluffy. Beat in egg. Add sifted dry ingredients and milk alternately. Shape dough into a 12″ roll and wrap in waxed paper. Chill until firm and slice into ⅛″ slices. Place on greased baking sheet. Bake 12 minutes in a 375° oven until light brown. Remove from baking sheet at once.

Yield: 5½ dozen

Peanut Cookies

1 cup salted peanuts
½ cup sweet butter, softened
¾ cup brown sugar, packed
1 egg
2 tsp. vanilla
1½ cups flour
½ tsp. salt

In a food processor, process half the peanuts with metal blade until it looks like peanut butter. Add butter, cut into 8 pats, add sugar, process until smooth; add egg and vanilla, process to mix well. Add remaining peanuts, flour and salt. Pulse 4 times, or until peanuts are chopped. Form the dough into two 7x2″ rolls, wrap well in waxed paper and chill overnight. Slice thin and bake on a lightly greased cookie sheet for 8-10 minutes in a 350° oven.

Yield: 8 dozen

Peanut-Butter Cocoas

¾ cup sweet butter, softened
½ cup chunky peanut butter
1 cup sugar
2 eggs
1 cup flour
¾ cup cocoa
1 tsp. baking powder
½ tsp. soda
¼ tsp. salt
6 oz. chocolate chips, chopped coarse

Cream together butter, peanut butter and sugar until light and fluffy. Beat in eggs one at a time. Sift together flour, cocoa, baking powder, soda and salt; combine with creamed mixture, blend. Add chocolate chips. Form dough into a roll 1½″ in diameter. Wrap in waxed paper and chill for 4 hours. Cut ¼″ slices, bake 1 inch apart on *ungreased* baking sheet in a 350° oven for 10-12 minutes, or until just firm to the touch.

Yield: 5 dozen

Crispy Pistachio Cookies

½ cup butter
1 cup sugar
1 egg
½ tsp. almond extract
½ tsp. grated orange peel
½ tsp. salt
1½ cups flour
½ tsp. baking powder
½ cup shelled, chopped pistachios

Cream butter and sugar until light and fluffy. Add egg, almond extract, orange peel and salt. Beat until smooth. Add flour, baking powder and pistachios. Mix thoroughly. Chill. Shape into a roll 2″ in diameter. Wrap and chill thoroughly. Slice ¼″ thick. Place on *ungreased* cookie sheet. Bake in a 400° oven for 6-8 minutes or until golden brown. Cool on rack.

Yield: 4½ dozen

Apple-Cider Cookies

½ cup sweet butter, softened
4 oz. cream cheese, softened
½ cup sugar
1 Tblsp. Calvados *or* cider
1 egg yolk
1¾ cups flour
¼ tsp. baking powder
¼ tsp. soda
⅛ tsp. salt
½ cup dried apples, chopped fine
sugar

Cream together butter, cream cheese and sugar; add Calvados and egg yolk, beating until smooth. Sift together flour, baking powder, soda and salt; combine dry ingredients to creamed mixture. Add the apples and mix. On a piece of waxed paper form the dough into a roll 1½″ in diameter. Sprinkle the roll with sugar, rolling to coat it thoroughly. Wrap in waxed paper and chill for 4 hours. Cut ⅜″ slices and bake 1 inch apart on *ungreased* baking sheets in a 350° oven for 10-12 minutes.

Yield: 5 dozen

Lemon-Nut Cookies

½ cup butter
½ cup margarine
½ cup brown sugar, packed
½ cup sugar
1 egg, beaten
1 Tblsp. fresh lemon juice
1 Tblsp. grated lemon peel
2 cups flour
¼ tsp. soda
¼ tsp. salt
½ cup ground walnuts

Cream butter and margarine; add sugars, egg, lemon juice and peel; mix well. Add sifted dry ingredients and nuts. Mix well. Form into rolls 2″ in diameter, wrap in waxed paper and chill overnight. Slice thin and bake in a 375° oven for 5-8 minutes on an *ungreased* cookie sheet.

Yield: 5 dozen

Fresh Ginger Cookies

½ cup blanched almonds
1½ cups flour
⅛ tsp. cloves
¼ tsp. ginger
½ tsp. cinnamon
⅛ tsp. nutmeg
½ tsp. soda
¼ tsp. salt
2 Tblsp. minced fresh ginger
½ cup sweet butter, softened, cut in eighths
½ cup dark brown sugar, packed
1 egg
2 Tblsp. molasses

Using a food processor, process almonds and ½ cup of flour, add remaining flour, cloves, ginger, cinnamon, nutmeg, soda and salt to mix. Transfer to waxed paper. Drop cut-up pieces of fresh ginger in machine while motor is running, measure 2 Tblsp. of fresh ginger, return to processor. Add butter and sugar, processing until smooth; add egg and molasses, process to mix. Add flour mixture, mix until well incorporated. Shape into 1x14″ roll, wrap in waxed paper, chill overnight. Slice thin and bake on a lightly greased cookie sheet 8-10 minutes in a 350° oven.

Yield: 12 dozen

BOEOTIAN (Tanagra), 5th century B.C.
Woman cooking; terracotta
Catharine Page Perkins Fund

Thin Molasses Cookies

¾ cup butter
½ cup molasses
½ cup brown sugar, packed
1½ cups flour
1½ tsp. ginger
½ tsp. soda
¼ tsp. *each* cloves, salt, allspice and cinnamon

Cream butter, molasses and sugar until light and fluffy. Sift dry ingredients and add to creamed mixture. Chill dough until firm enough to handle. Form into two 6″ rolls and wrap in waxed paper. Chill overnight. Cut ¼″ slices and arrange 2 inches apart on an *ungreased* cookie sheet. Bake in a 375° oven for 6-8 minutes.

Yield: 5 dozen

Orange-Apricot Cookies

peel of 1 small orange
½ cup dried apricots
1½ cups flour
½ cup sweet butter
¾ cup brown sugar, packed
1 egg
1 tsp. vanilla
¼ tsp. salt

Remove orange peel with swivel-bladed peeler. Using food processor, chop orange peel and apricots with ½ cup of flour until finely chopped; set aside. Cut butter into 8 pats, process with sugar, add egg and vanilla. Add remaining ingredients, mix until well incorporated. Shape into two 9″ rolls. Slice thin and bake on a greased baking sheet 1 inch apart in a 350° oven for 8-10 minutes.

Yield: 7 dozen

Rolled Cookies

Rolled cookies are made from dough stiff enough to roll thin with a rolling pin. Before baking, dough is cut into desired shapes.

The dough is usually chilled at least 15-30 minutes before rolling so that it will be easier to handle without the addition of too much flour. Roll out only a small amount of dough on a lightly floured surface. Roll dough from the center to the edges with as few motions as possible to the desired thickness. Dip cookie cutter in flour, shake off excess, and lift cut dough to cookie sheet. Set aside cookie trimmings and roll again separately; these will be less tender because of the extra flour and handling.

Rolled cookies should be uniformly shaped, tender and fine in texture, and lightly browned. Depending on type, cookies will be either thin and crisp or thicker and soft.

Windmill Cookies

8 oz. cream cheese, softened
¾ cup sweet butter, softened
1 egg yolk
1½ cups flour
1 Tblsp. baking powder
½ cup strawberry jam
confectioners' sugar

Beat cream cheese, butter and egg yolk until smooth. Blend in flour and baking powder to form stiff dough. Divide in half. Wrap in plastic wrap and refrigerate 1 hour. Roll out half of dough between 2 sheets of plastic wrap to thickness of ⅛″. Cut into 3″ squares. Transfer to *ungreased* baking sheets. On each square, make cut from each corner almost to center. Fold every other corner to center and press to seal. Place about 1 tsp. jam in center of windmill. Bake until golden, about 15 minutes in a 350° oven. Transfer to rack. Repeat with remaining dough. Let cookies cool completely. Sift confectioners' sugar lightly over cookies. Store in airtight container.

Yield: 2 dozen

Tea Wafers

½ cup butter
½ cup Crisco
1½ cups sugar
2 eggs, beaten
½ tsp. soda
3 Tblsp. sour cream
3 cups flour
¼ tsp. salt

Cream butter and Crisco with sugar. Add eggs, beat well. Dissolve soda in sour cream. Add to egg mixture together with flour and salt. Mix well. Chill dough until stiff. Roll dough on floured surface until very thin. Work fast, before dough softens. Cut into desired shapes. Place on greased cookie sheet. Bake in a 400° oven about 5 minutes, until light brown. Sprinkle with sugar *or* cinnamon and sugar, if desired.

Yield: 5 dozen

Soft Molasses Cookies

½ cup butter
½ cup sugar
½ cup buttermilk
1 cup molasses
1 egg
5 cups flour
1½ tsp. soda
1¼ tsp. salt
1 Tblsp. ginger
⅛ tsp. cayenne pepper

Cream butter and sugar. Add buttermilk, molasses and egg, beat well. Sift together dry ingredients and stir into creamed mixture. Dough will be stiff, yet soft. Chill until firm. Roll on floured surface ¼″ thick, sprinkle with sugar. Cut into squares, diamonds, gingerbread figures or fancy shapes. Place on lightly greased cookie sheets. Bake in a 350° oven for 7-10 minutes. Stays moist and mellows with age.

Yield: 6 dozen

Cinnamon Roll-Ups

1 cup butter
2 cups flour
1 egg yolk
¾ cup sour cream
¾ cup sugar
¾ cup finely chopped nuts
1 tsp. cinnamon
1 egg white, slightly beaten
1 Tblsp. water

Cut butter into flour until mixture resembles coarse crumbs. Stir in egg yolk and sour cream. Mix. Chill dough for 1-2 hours. Combine sugar, nuts and cinnamon. Divide dough into quarters. Roll each quarter into 11″ circle on floured surface. Sprinkle with ¼ nut-sugar mixture. Cut into 16 wedges. Roll up starting at widest end. Place rolls, about 2 inches apart, on *ungreased* baking sheets. Brush with combined egg white and water. Bake in 350° oven until golden brown about 20 minutes.

Yield: 5 dozen

German Sand Tarts

1 cup butter
1¼ cups sugar
2 cups flour
1 egg, beaten
1 egg white
1 Tblsp. sugar
¼ tsp. cinnamon
30 pecan halves

Cream butter and sugar. Add flour slowly, working it in as for pastry. Add beaten egg and mix well. Chill thoroughly. Roll to ⅛″ thick, cut rounds and place on a lightly greased cookie sheet. Brush lightly with egg white beaten until frothy. Sprinkle with sugar and cinnamon. Place pecan half firmly in the center of each cookie. Bake for 8-12 minutes in a 375° oven.

Yield: 2½ dozen

Lemon Hearts

3 egg yolks
⅔ cup sugar
1 tsp. vanilla
2¼ cups finely ground almonds
⅛ tsp. lemon extract
⅛ tsp. baking powder
sugar

Beat egg yolks, sugar and vanilla until thick and lemon colored. Stir in half the almonds, lemon extract and baking powder. Transfer dough to well-sugared surface, knead in enough of the remaining almonds to form soft dough. Shape into ball. Refrigerate wrapped in plastic wrap until cold, about 1½ hours. Line baking sheets with greased foil. Roll dough on lightly sugared surface ¼″ thick. Cut out cookies with 2″ heart-shaped cutter. Place on baking sheets. Bake until edges are golden, 8-10 minutes in a 400° oven.

Lemon Icing:
1-1½ Tblsp. lemon juice
1 cup confectioners' sugar

Beat lemon juice into sugar in small bowl until the consistency of corn syrup. Spread on warm cookies. Cool on racks.

Yield: 4½ dozen

Orange Thins

½ cup butter
1 cup sugar
2 eggs
2½ cups flour
1 Tblsp. baking powder
¼ tsp. salt
½ cup orange juice

Cream butter and sugar. Add eggs. Sift together dry ingredients and add alternating with orange juice. Roll to about ⅛″ thick. Cut. Place on a slightly greased baking sheet and bake in a 400° oven for 8-10 minutes.

Yield: 4 dozen

FRENCH (Sèvres), 1761
Tea or breakfast service; soft-paste porcelain
Gift of Rita and Frits Markus

Bavarian Almond Cookies

1 cup sweet butter, softened
1 cup confectioners' sugar
2 egg yolks
2¼ cups flour
⅛ tsp. nutmeg
⅛ tsp. cinnamon
⅛ tsp. cloves
1 cup finely ground almonds
1 egg white, lightly beaten
¾ cup slivered blanched almonds
1 cup apricot preserves

Cream butter and sugar; beat in egg yolks. Gradually beat in flour, nutmeg, cinnamon and cloves, which have been sifted together. Stir in ground almonds until dough almost cleans side of bowl. Shape dough into ball; wrap in plastic wrap. Refrigerate covered 2 hours. Divide dough in half. Roll one piece on lightly floured surface ⅛" thick. Cut out cookies with 2½" doughnut cutter to make rings. Roll remaining dough and cut out 2½" circles. Place rings and circles on greased foil-lined baking sheets. Refrigerate covered 1 hour. Brush rings with egg white. Press slivered almonds into rings. Bake rings and circles in a 350° oven for 10-12 minutes, until edges are light brown. Cool completely on racks. Spread circles generously with apricot preserves; top with rings, almond side up. Store between sheets of waxed paper in airtight container.

Yield: 2½ dozen

Butterscotch Cookies

2 cups flour
2 tsp. baking powder
dash salt
½ cup butter
1⅓ cups brown sugar, packed
1 egg
1 tsp. vanilla
2 Tblsp. evaporated milk

Sift together flour, baking powder and salt; set aside. Cream butter and brown sugar until light and fluffy. Beat in egg and vanilla. Add flour mixture alternately with milk. Knead until well blended. Cover and chill for 1 hour. On lightly floured surface roll to ⅛" thickness. Cut into desired shapes with floured cookie cutter. Bake on a greased baking sheet for 10 minutes in a 400° oven, until brown. Remove from baking sheet at once.

Yield: 5 dozen

Crisp Molasses Cookies

½ cup butter, melted
1 cup molasses, heated
½ cup brown sugar, packed
¼ tsp. nutmeg
¾ tsp. ginger
¾ tsp. cloves
¾ tsp. cinnamon
¼ tsp. allspice
¼ tsp. salt
1 tsp. soda
3 cups flour

Combine butter, heated molasses, sugar, spices, salt and soda. Add flour and mix thoroughly. Form into ball, wrap in plastic wrap and chill 1 hour. Roll very thin and cut into desired shapes. Place cookies on *ungreased* baking sheet and bake in a 375° oven for 7-8 minutes.

Yield: 5 dozen

Chocolate Sticks

1 egg
1 egg yolk
1⅔ cups sugar
2¼ cups finely ground almonds
⅔ cup grated semi-sweet chocolate
sugar

Beat egg and egg yolk until foamy; gradually beat in sugar, beat until thick and lemon colored. Fold in almonds and chocolate; shape dough into ball. Refrigerate, wrapped in plastic wrap until cold, about 1½ hours. Line baking sheets with foil. Roll dough on lightly sugared surface ¼" thick. Cut into 2x¾" sticks. Place on baking sheets; bake in a 350° oven until centers are firm to the touch and edges are light brown, 10-12 minutes. Slide foil onto racks and cool.

Yield: 5-6 dozen

Chocolate Cinnamon Cookies

3 oz. unsweetened chocolate
2 cups sifted cake flour
1½ tsp. baking powder
½ tsp. soda
1 tsp. cinnamon
½ tsp. salt
½ cup butter
1 cup sugar
1 egg
2 Tblsp. milk
sugar

Melt chocolate over warm water; set aside to cool. Sift together cake flour, baking powder, soda, cinnamon and salt; set aside. Cream together butter and sugar until light and fluffy. Add egg and beat well. Add chocolate and milk, blend thoroughly. Stir in dry ingredients, mixing well. Wrap in plastic wrap and chill dough overnight. Divide dough in half. Roll out on lightly floured surface to ⅛" thickness. Cut into fancy shapes. Place 2 inches apart on *ungreased* baking sheets. Sprinkle with sugar. Bake 8-10 minutes in a 350° oven.

Yield: 4 dozen

Sugar Cookies

1 cup butter
4 cups flour
1½ cups sugar
½ tsp. salt
1 tsp. soda
2 eggs, beaten
4 Tblsp. milk
1 tsp. vanilla

Cut butter into flour; add sugar, salt and soda. Mix eggs, milk and vanilla; add to flour-butter mixture. Roll ⅛″ thick, cut into desired shapes, brush with milk and sprinkle with sugar. Bake on a greased cookie sheet in a 350° oven for 8-10 minutes.

Yield: 7 dozen

Springerle

4 eggs
1 lb. confectioners' sugar
6 Tblsp. butter, melted
grated peel of 1 lemon
1 tsp. anise oil
2-3 tsp. anise seeds
4 cups flour
2 tsp. baking powder
½ tsp. salt

Stir eggs and sugar together, beating well for ½ hour in electric mixer. Add melted butter, lemon peel, anise oil and anise seeds. Sift together flour, baking powder and salt, add and mix well. Roll dough on lightly floured surface ½″ thick. Then roll with a floured springerle rolling pin. Cut cookies apart so each cookie has a design. Generously grease baking sheets, transfer cookies printed side up, and allow to stand uncovered at room temperature overnight. Bake in a 325° oven 10-15 minutes, until brown. Cool on rack. Texture and flavor improve if allowed to age in airtight container for a week.

Yield: 4-5 dozen

Christmas Honey Cookies

1 cup butter
1 cup sugar
1 cup honey
2 Tblsp. hot water
1 tsp. soda
½ tsp. cardamom
3¾ cups flour
blanched almond halves

Cream butter and sugar, add honey and cream thoroughly. Add hot water to creamed mixture. Add sifted dry ingredients. Roll to ⅛″ thick and cut in squares. Place on lightly greased cookie sheet; set almond halves in center. Bake for 10-12 minutes in 350° oven.

Yield: 7 dozen

Mexican Holiday Cookies

2¼ cups butter
1 cup sweet white wine *or* fruit juice
2 cups sugar
2 Tblsp. + 1 tsp. cinnamon
1 Tblsp. anise seeds
2 egg yolks
4 cups flour

Cream butter. Combine wine, 1 cup sugar, 1 Tblsp. cinnamon and anise seeds in a small bowl. Gradually beat wine mixture into butter. Beat in egg yolks, one at a time, beating well after each addition. Stir in flour. Refrigerate dough overnight. Roll dough ⅜″ thick on a lightly floured surface. Cut out circles with 1″ round cutter. Place on greased baking sheets and bake in a 350° oven for 15-20 minutes, until golden brown. Combine remaining 1 cup sugar and 1 Tblsp. + 1 tsp. cinnamon. Dip hot cookies into sugar mixture to coat. Cool on racks. Store in airtight container up to one week.

Yield: 8 dozen

Breads

There are proper processes for handling different types of bread. When bread is made with baking powder and soda, the quick leavening agents, it is a quick bread and easy to make. The usual method of preparation is to combine shortening, egg, and liquid, then to stir in the dry ingredients only enough to dampen the flour. Quick breads should be free from tunnels, with uniform, medium texture; they should be light and tender, of moist crumb, and golden brown, with an evenly rounded, pebbly surface.

Scones and biscuits contain larger amounts of shortening and are mixed in the same manner as pastry, cutting shortening into flour mixture with cold liquid added quickly and lightly. This method produces a fine flaky texture.

Yeast bread is made with a living organism, which leavens and gives a distinctive flavor. To prevent destruction of yeast action by heat, any ingredient mixed with yeast should be lukewarm. The object of kneading is to develop elasticity of gluten and scatter gas pockets that have formed around the yeast, which insures uniformity of texture. When the dough becomes non-sticky, feels springy and elastic, and looks satiny smooth it has been kneaded sufficiently. Temperature during the rising period is most satisfactory for the dough around 80°, the bowl covered with a cloth to protect from drafts and to prevent drying. When dough is too warm, bread will have a dark color, coarse texture, yeasty flavor, and a dry, flat top. When dough is too cold, bread will be heavy, solid, and low in volume. The desired final product is well raised, uniform in texture, slightly moist, and springy with a light brown crust.

Christmas-Pudding Bread

8 oz. mixed candied fruits
2 oz. candied pineapple pieces
½ cup golden raisins
½ cup dark raisins
¼ cup port
¼ cup brandy
2¼ cups sifted cake flour
¾ tsp. soda
¼ tsp. cinnamon
¼ tsp. allspice
¼ tsp. nutmeg
¼ tsp. salt
grated peel of 1 lemon
grated peel of 1 small orange
¼ cup sugar
¾ cup dark brown sugar, packed
¼ cup sweet butter, melted
⅓ cup vegetable oil
¼ cup dark molasses
3 eggs
½ cup canned purple plums, drained and cut up

Mix chopped candied fruits, pineapple pieces, raisins, port and brandy in a bowl; let stand 2 hours. Sift together flour, soda, spices and salt; set aside. Combine grated lemon and orange peel with sugars. Add butter and oil, cream well. Add molasses and eggs, one at a time. Add plums and blend well. Add half the dry ingredients and ½ of the candied fruits. Stir gently. Add remaining dry ingredients and fruits, mix until flour is moistened. Pour into a well-greased 9x5x3-inch loaf pan, lined with waxed paper and greased again. Bake in a 300° oven for 60-80 minutes, or until tester comes out clean. Cool on rack for 30 minutes, remove loaf from pan. Wrap in aluminum foil and refrigerate 2 days before serving. Can be stored in refrigerator up to 2 weeks.

Yield: 1 loaf

Raisin-Date-Nut Bread

3/4 cup dark raisins
1/4 cup golden raisins
1 cup pitted dates, quartered
1 cup boiling water
1/2 cup butter, softened
1 cup sugar
1 egg
1 tsp. vanilla
1 1/3 cups flour
1 tsp. soda
3/4 cup coarsely chopped walnuts

Place raisins and dates in a bowl and pour water over fruits. Cream butter and sugar until light and fluffy. Beat in egg and vanilla. Sift together flour and soda; add and mix well. Carefully stir in the fruit mixture and walnuts. The batter will be very liquid. Pour the mixture into a 9x5x3-inch greased loaf pan that has been lined on the bottom with a greased rectangle of waxed paper. Bake for 60-70 minutes in a 350° oven or until a tester inserted in the center comes out clean. Let cool for 5 minutes. Invert onto rack and remove paper. Cool thoroughly before slicing.

Yield: 1 loaf

Tea-Lime Bread

1 tea bag
boiling water
2 eggs
2/3 cup sugar
1/2 cup butter, melted
grated peel of 2 limes
3/4 cup unblanched almonds, finely chopped
1 1/3 cups sifted cake flour
1 tsp. baking powder
1/4 tsp. soda
1/4 tsp. salt

Place tea bag in 1 cup glass measure, add boiling water to measure 1/2 cup. Steep until lukewarm, squeeze and discard tea bag. Beat eggs until frothy, add sugar, mix well. Slowly add hot, melted butter and continue beating until thoroughly blended. Add lime peel, almonds and tea. Sift together dry ingredients and mix until flour is moistened. Pour batter into greased and floured 9x5x3-inch loaf pan. Bake in 325° oven, on center rack for about 45 minutes. Cool in pan on wire rack for 15 minutes before removing from pan.

Yield: 1 loaf

Orange-Nut Bread

2 1/4 cups flour
2 tsp. baking powder
1/2 tsp. soda
3/4 tsp. salt
3/4 cup + 2 Tblsp. sugar
3/4 cup chopped nuts
1/2 cup raisins
1/4 cup grated orange peel
1 egg, beaten
1/2 cup milk
1/2 cup orange juice
2 Tblsp. butter, melted

Sift flour with baking powder, soda, salt and sugar. Add nuts, raisins and orange peel. Combine egg, milk and orange juice; add to flour mixture with melted butter. Mix until flour is moistened and fruit distributed. Pour into a greased 9x5x3-inch loaf pan. Bake for 1 hour in a 350° oven, or until top springs back when pressed lightly. Cool, wrap in foil, store overnight before slicing.

Yield: 1 loaf

Pineapple-Orange Bread

2 cups whole-wheat flour
1½ tsp. baking powder
½ tsp. soda
1 tsp. salt
1 cup crushed canned pineapple, drained
½ cup chopped walnuts
2 tsp. grated orange peel
1 egg, beaten
½ cup honey
¾ cup fresh orange juice
2 Tblsp. vegetable oil

Sift together flour, baking powder, soda and salt. Stir in pineapple, nuts and peel; set aside. Combine egg, honey, orange juice and oil, add to dry ingredients; stir only until moistened. Bake in a greased 9x5x3-inch loaf pan. Bake in a 350° oven for 50 minutes. Remove from pan and cool on a rack. Wrap in foil and store overnight before slicing.

Yield: 1 loaf

Date-Nut Bread

1 cup boiling water
16 oz. pitted dates, halved
1 Tblsp. Crisco
1½ cups flour
1 cup sugar
1 tsp. salt
1 tsp. soda
1 egg, slightly beaten
1 tsp. vanilla
1 cup chopped walnuts or pecans

In a large mixing bowl pour boiling water over dates and shortening to soften dates and melt shortening. Sift together flour, sugar, salt and soda; set aside. Add egg and vanilla to date mixture. Stir in dry ingredients. Fold in nuts. Pour into two well-greased 7x3x2-inch loaf pans, bake in a 325° oven for 45-50 minutes or until tester comes out clean.

Yield: 2 medium loaves

Fresh Strawberry Bread

¾ cup butter
½ cup vegetable oil
1½ cups brown sugar, packed
4 eggs
1¼ cups whole-wheat flour
2 cups flour
1 tsp. cinnamon (optional)
1 tsp. salt
¾ tsp. soda
2 cups fresh strawberries, chopped
1 cup pecans, chopped

Cream butter and oil, beat until oil is emulsified. Add brown sugar and cream well. Beat in the eggs, one at a time. Sift together flours, cinnamon, salt and soda; add, stirring only until dry ingredients are moistened. Gently fold in strawberries and pecans. Pour into a well-greased 9x5x3-inch loaf pan and bake for 50-60 minutes in a 350° oven.

Yield: 1 loaf

Pear Bread

½ cup sweet butter, softened
1 cup sugar
2 eggs
1 tsp. vanilla
2 cups flour
½ tsp. salt
½ tsp. soda
1 tsp. baking powder
pinch nutmeg
¼ cup buttermilk
1 cup coarsely chopped pears
½ cup chopped nuts (optional)

Cream butter, add sugar and beat until light and fluffy. Add eggs and vanilla and beat well. Sift together flour, salt, soda, baking powder, nutmeg; add alternately with buttermilk. Do not overmix. Gently fold in pears and nuts. Pour into a well-greased 9x5x3-inch loaf pan. Bake in a 350° oven for 50-60 minutes.

Yield: 1 loaf

EGYPTIAN, late 18th Dynasty, 1300 B.C.
Mummy cloth; gessoed linen
William Stevenson Smith Fund

Cherry-Almond Bread

3 cups flour
1¼ tsp. salt
1 tsp. soda
2 tsp. baking powder
1 cup chopped almonds
¼ cup sweet butter
1 cup + 1 tsp. sugar
2 eggs, lightly beaten
1 cup buttermilk
1 tsp. almond extract
1 cup canned sour cherries, drained and coarsely chopped
2 Tblsp. sliced almonds

Combine flour, salt, soda, baking powder and chopped almonds. Set aside. Cream butter and 1 cup sugar; add eggs, mix well. Stir in buttermilk and almond extract, mix well. Add the dry ingredients and stir only until moistened. Fold in cherries gently. Pour batter in a greased 9x5x3-inch loaf pan. Sprinkle with sliced almonds and 1 tsp. sugar. Bake in a 350° oven for 60-70 minutes, or until a tester comes out clean. Cool in pan for 10 minutes before removing. Cool thoroughly before wrapping. Best if served warm.

Yield: 1 loaf

Hawaiian Bread

1 cup vegetable oil
2 cups sugar
3 eggs
2½ cups flour
1 tsp. salt
1 tsp. soda
1 tsp. cinnamon
2 tsp. vanilla
1 cup crushed canned pineapple, drained
1 cup grated coconut
2 cups raw grated carrots

Cream oil, sugar and eggs until light. Sift together flour, salt, soda and cinnamon, add to creamed mixture. Gently fold in vanilla, pineapple, coconut and carrots. Divide batter between 2 well-greased 9x5x3-inch loaf pans. Let batter rest 20-30 minutes, then bake in a 350° oven for 60 minutes.

Yield: 2 loaves

Apple-Pecan Loaf

4 cups peeled, diced apples
1 cup broken pecans
2 cups sugar
3 cups flour
2 tsp. soda
½ tsp. salt
¼ tsp. *each* allspice, nutmeg and cinnamon
1 cup sweet butter, melted
1 tsp. vanilla
2 eggs, well beaten

Topping:
2 tsp. sugar
½ tsp. cinnamon

Combine apples, pecans, 2 cups sugar, let stand one hour. Stir often. Sift together dry ingredients and add to apples. Melt butter, add vanilla and combine with apple mixture and eggs. Grease a 9x5x3-inch loaf pan, line with waxed paper, grease again. Pour batter into pan, bake for 90 minutes in a 325° oven. Mix together remaining 2 tsp. sugar and ½ tsp. cinnamon, dust over top of batter for last half-hour of baking. Remove from oven, let cool in pan for 45 minutes. Do not slice until thoroughly cool.

Yield: 1 loaf

Mango Bread

3/4 cup pecan pieces
2 Tblsp. sweet butter, melted
peel of 1 medium orange
3/4 cup sugar
1 3/4 cups flour
1 1/2 tsp. baking powder
1 tsp. cinnamon
1/2 tsp. salt
1/2 tsp. nutmeg
1/4 tsp. soda
1/3 cup vegetable oil
1/4 cup buttermilk
1 egg
1 tsp. vanilla
1 medium mango, peeled and cut into 1/2-inch cubes

Chop pecans coarse with the metal blade of a food processor. Brown in 1 Tblsp. butter over medium heat about 3 minutes. Set aside. Process the orange peel and sugar until peel is fine. Add flour, baking powder, cinnamon, salt, nutmeg and soda, process until combined. Mix oil, buttermilk, egg, vanilla and remaining Tblsp. butter, add to batter and process until absorbed. Remove to a large bowl and fold in the mango. Pour into a greased 9x5x3-inch pan, lined on the bottom with waxed paper. Smooth the top and press pecans on top. Bake in a 350° oven for 60-65 minutes, or until a tester comes out clean.

Glaze:
1/3 cup confectioners' sugar
1 Tblsp. light cream
1 tsp. vanilla

Combine the confectioners' sugar, cream and vanilla in a small bowl. Pour over the bread while it is still hot and set aside for 10 minutes. Remove from pan and cool for 8 hours before cutting.

Yield: 1 loaf

Caribbean Banana Bread

1 cup currants
1/2 cup dark rum
3 cups flour
1 tsp. salt
1 tsp. soda
1 tsp. baking powder
2 tsp. cinnamon
1/2 tsp. nutmeg
1/2 cup + 2 Tblsp. flaked coconut
1/2 cup sweet butter
1 cup dark brown sugar, packed
2 eggs, lightly beaten
1/3 cup buttermilk
1 cup mashed ripe banana

Steep the currants and rum, heated, for 1 hour. Combine flour, salt, soda, baking powder, cinnamon, nutmeg and 1/2 cup coconut. Set aside. Cream together butter, sugar and eggs; mix well. Stir in buttermilk, banana and currant mixture, combining well. Add dry ingredients and stir until moistened. Pour batter into a greased 9x5x3-inch loaf pan and sprinkle with remaining 2 Tblsp. coconut. Bake in a 350° oven for 60-70 minutes, or until tester comes out clean. Cool on rack for 10 minutes before removing from pan. Cool thoroughly before wrapping. Best if served warm.

Yield: 1 loaf

Applesauce-Nut Bread

2 cups flour
2 tsp. baking powder
½ tsp. soda
½ tsp. salt
1 tsp. cinnamon
¼ tsp. nutmeg
½ cup coarsely chopped pecans
1 egg, lightly beaten
½ cup brown sugar, packed
1 Tblsp. lemon juice
½ cup evaporated milk
1 cup applesauce
3 Tblsp. butter, melted

Sift flour with baking powder, soda, salt and spices. Stir in nuts. Set aside. Lightly beat egg, add sugar; beat until light and creamy. Add lemon juice to milk, mix with creamed mixture, add applesauce and butter. Add dry ingredients and stir only to blend. Pour into a greased 9x5x3-inch loaf pan. Bake in a 350° oven for 60 minutes.

Yield: 1 loaf

Fresh Apple Bread

½ cup butter
1 cup sugar
2 eggs
2 Tblsp. buttermilk
2 cups flour
1 tsp. soda
½ tsp. salt
2 cups peeled, chopped apples
½ cup chopped nuts
Topping:
2 Tblsp. sugar
2 Tblsp. flour
2 Tblsp. melted butter

Cream butter and sugar, add eggs and continue creaming until light. Add buttermilk. Sift together dry ingredients and blend to moisten. Fold in apples and nuts. Pour into a greased 9x5x3-inch loaf pan. Combine ingredients for topping and spread over batter. Bake for 60-75 minutes, until tester comes out clean, in a 350° oven. Cool in pan for 10 minutes before removing. Cool before slicing.

Yield: 1 loaf

Spiced Apple Bread

1½ cups flour
1 cup whole-wheat flour
1 tsp. salt
1 tsp. soda
1 tsp. baking powder
2 tsp. cinnamon
¼ tsp. ginger
¼ tsp. nutmeg
3 Tblsp. sweet butter
⅔ cup brown sugar, packed
2 eggs, lightly beaten
1 cup buttermilk
½ cups chopped pecans
1 apple, peeled and chopped

Sift together flours, salt, soda, baking powder, cinnamon, ginger and nutmeg. Set aside. Cream butter, brown sugar and eggs; mix well. Stir in buttermilk combining mixture thoroughly. Add dry ingredients, pecans and apple; stir until moistened. Pour batter into 2 greased 7x3x2-inch loaf pans. Bake in a 350° oven for 45-50 minutes, or until a tester comes out clean. Cool on rack for 10 minutes before removing from pans. Cool for 2 hours before wrapping. Best if served warm.

Yield: 2 medium loaves

Cranberry Lemon Bread

2 cups flour
1 tsp. salt
1 tsp. soda
1 tsp. baking powder
¼ cup sweet butter
1¼ cups sugar
2 eggs, lightly beaten
½ cup buttermilk
½ tsp. vanilla
1 Tblsp. grated lemon peel
1 cup cranberries (fresh or frozen)

Sift together flour, salt, soda, baking powder; set aside. Cream butter and sugar, add eggs, beat well. Stir in buttermilk, vanilla and lemon peel; combine well. Add dry ingredients, mix just until moistened. Fold in cranberries. Pour batter into 9x5x3-inch greased loaf pan, bake in a 350° oven 60 minutes, or until tester comes out clean. Cool in pan on rack for 10 minutes. Loosen edges with a knife, remove from pan and cool for 2 hours. Wrap well in foil. Best served warm.

Yield: 1 loaf

Cranberry Quick Bread

1¾ cups flour
1 cup sugar
1 Tblsp. baking powder
¾ tsp. salt
½ tsp. cinnamon
1 egg, lightly beaten
1 Tblsp. grated orange peel
¾ cup milk
2 Tblsp. butter, melted
1 cup fresh cranberries, chopped

Sift together first five ingredients into a bowl; set aside. Mix the egg with orange peel, milk and butter. Pour over the dry ingredients. Mix until just moistened. Stir in cranberries. Spoon into a well-greased 8x4x3-inch loaf pan. Bake in a 325° oven 1 hour, or until a tester inserted in center comes out clean.

Yield: 1 loaf

Cranberry Mincemeat Bread

2 cups cranberry mincemeat
½ cup sweet butter, cut in pieces
1 cup sugar
2 eggs
2 cups flour
1 tsp. baking powder
½ tsp. salt
½ tsp. soda

Prepare cranberry mincemeat and *allow one week to mellow.* Cream butter and sugar in processor until light and fluffy, add eggs and combine well. Sift together dry ingredients, add and process until just combined. Add mincemeat. Pour into greased 9x5x3-inch pan. Bake in a 350° oven 60-70 minutes, until tester comes out clean. Cool in pan for 5 minutes and turn out on rack to cool completely.

Yield: 1 loaf

Cranberry Mincemeat:

½ cup cranberries
½ cup raisins
½ cup golden raisins
½ cup currants
4 oz. dried apples
4 oz. dried apricots
¾ tsp. cinnamon
¼ tsp. salt
⅛ tsp. nutmeg
⅛ tsp. allspice
⅛ tsp. freshly ground pepper
1 cup dark rum
1 cup apple cider *or* apple juice
½ cup dark brown sugar, packed
¼ cup sweet butter, cut in pieces
3 Tblsp. light molasses

Combine fruit and seasonings in food processor or blender and chop until coarse. Heat rum, apple cider, brown sugar, butter and molasses until butter is melted. Pour over coarsely chopped fruit, mix well, refrigerate, covered, for at least 1 week to mellow.

Yield: 4 cups

LUIS MELENDEZ (Italian, 1716–1780)
Still Life with Melon and Pears; oil painting, ca. 1770
Margaret Curry Wyman Fund

Apricot Nut Bread

1 cup dried apricots
1 cup sugar
2 Tblsp. melted butter
1 egg
2 cups flour
1 tsp. baking powder
$\frac{1}{4}$ tsp. soda
1 tsp. salt
$\frac{1}{4}$ cup water
$\frac{1}{2}$ cup orange juice
$\frac{1}{2}$ cup chopped walnuts

Cover apricots with warm water and soak for 30 minutes. Drain and cut into small pieces. Cream together sugar, butter and egg. Sift together dry ingredients and add alternately to creamed mixture with water and orange juice; mix only until dry ingredients are moistened. Fold in apricots and walnuts. Pour batter into greased and floured 9x5x3-inch loaf pan. Bake in a 350° oven for 55-60 minutes. Cool in pan.

Yield: 1 loaf

Pumpkin Bread

$\frac{2}{3}$ cup butter
$2\frac{2}{3}$ cups sugar
4 eggs
$15\frac{1}{2}$-oz. can pumpkin
$\frac{2}{3}$ cup orange juice
$3\frac{1}{2}$ cups flour
2 tsp. soda
$1\frac{1}{2}$ tsp. salt
$\frac{1}{2}$ tsp. baking powder
1 tsp. cinnamon
1 tsp. cloves
$\frac{2}{3}$ cup chopped nuts
$\frac{2}{3}$ cup raisins

Cream butter and sugar well, until light. Add eggs, one at a time. Add pumpkin and juice; blend well. Stir in dry ingredients until mixture is moistened. Gently fold in nuts and raisins. Pour batter in two greased 9x5x3-inch loaf pans, bake in a 350° oven for 65-75 minutes, or until tester comes out clean.

Variation:
$\frac{2}{3}$ cup water
$\frac{2}{3}$ cup dates, chopped

Substitute for orange juice and raisins. Eliminate nuts.

Yield: 2 loaves

Zucchini Bread

2 cups coarsely grated zucchini
3 eggs, well beaten
2 cups sugar
1 cup vegetable oil
1 Tblsp. vanilla
2 cups flour
1 Tblsp. cinnamon
2 tsp. soda
1 tsp. salt
$\frac{1}{4}$ tsp. baking powder
1 cup nuts, broken

Sprinkle zucchini with salt in colander. Weight with plate and let drain 1 hour. Squeeze out excess moisture. Beat eggs until frothy. Add sugar, oil and vanilla; beat until thick and lemon colored. Stir in zucchini, then sifted dry ingredients. Fold in nuts. Pour into two greased and floured 9x5x3-inch loaf pans. Bake for 45-60 minutes, or until a tester comes out clean, in a 350° oven.

Yield: 2 loaves

Mini Orange Muffins

2 cups flour
1 tsp. soda
1 cup butter
1 cup sugar
2 eggs
1 cup buttermilk
grated peel of 2 oranges
½ cup golden raisins
juice of 2 oranges
1 cup brown sugar, packed

Sift together flour and soda; set aside. Cream butter and sugar, add eggs and beat until well blended. Add buttermilk, orange peel and raisins. Add dry ingredients and stir only enough to dampen the flour. Fill well-greased miniature muffin pans two-thirds full and bake in a 400° oven for 15-20 minutes. Mix orange juice with brown sugar. Spoon mixture over muffins. Immediately remove from pan.

Yield: 5 dozen miniature

Refrigerator Bran Muffins

5 cups flour
5 tsp. soda
2 tsp. salt
2½ cups sugar
8 cups raisin bran cereal
1 cup vegetable oil
4 eggs, beaten
1 quart buttermilk

Sift together flour, soda and salt into large mixing bowl. Blend sugar and bran cereal with other dry ingredients. Add oil, eggs and buttermilk; mix well. Store in covered container and keep in refrigerator up to 6 weeks. For muffins, fill greased tins ⅔ full and bake in a 400° oven 15-20 minutes.

Yield: 4-5 dozen

Sugary Blueberry Muffins

2 Tblsp. butter
1½ cups sugar
2 eggs
½ cup milk
1½ cups flour
2 tsp. baking powder
1 tsp. salt
2 cups blueberries, fresh or frozen

Cream together butter and sugar until well blended. Beat in eggs. Add milk and mix. Sift together flour, baking powder and salt. Add dry ingredients and stir until moistened. Do not overmix; batter should be lumpy. Carefully fold in blueberries. (If unthawed frozen blueberries are used, coat with 2 tsp. flour before folding into batter.) Fill well-greased muffin tins ⅔ full. Bake in a 400° oven for 25-30 minutes.

Yield: 1½ dozen

Scottish Bannocks

1½ cups flour
1 cup quick oatmeal
¼ cup butter, softened
2 Tblsp. sugar
1 Tblsp. baking powder
pinch salt
⅓-½ cup milk

Combine flour, oatmeal, butter, sugar, baking powder and salt in a large bowl. Work mixture against side of bowl with wooden spoon until butter is completely blended. Slowly stir in enough milk to make stiff dough. Turn out onto a lightly floured surface and quickly knead just until dough holds together. Roll dough out ½″ thick. Cut into 2″ rounds. Arrange on ungreased baking sheet 1 inch apart. Bake in a 425° oven until light brown, 12-15 minutes. Serve hot, or cool on racks. May be split and toasted.

Yield: 1 dozen

Butterhorns

1 cup butter
12 oz. small-curd cottage cheese
2 cups flour
dash salt

Cream butter and cottage cheese in large mixing bowl. Add flour and salt. Refrigerate 4 hours or overnight. Divide dough into 3 parts. Roll each part in circle on floured board. Cut circle into 12 wedges. Roll into butterhorns, starting the roll at wide end and rolling to point. Place on greased cookie sheet. Bake 30-40 minutes in a 350° oven. Frost with butter cream frosting.

Yield: 3 dozen

Fruit-and-Cream Scones

1¾ cups flour
1 Tblsp. sugar
2½ tsp. baking powder
¼ tsp. salt
2 eggs
⅓ cup heavy cream
3 Tblsp. fresh orange juice
1 Tblsp. grated orange peel
½ cup dates, chopped

Sift together flour, sugar, baking powder and salt into large mixing bowl; set aside. In small bowl beat together eggs and cream, reserve 1 Tblsp. of the mixture. Stir in orange juice and peel. Add orange juice mixture and dates to dry ingredients. Stir lightly with a fork until a sticky, soft dough is formed. Knead the dough lightly on a floured surface for 30 seconds. Pat it gently to ¾″ thick. Cut into rounds, triangles or diamond shapes. Place on greased baking sheets. Brush the tops with reserved egg mixture and bake in a 425° oven for 12-15 minutes, until golden.

Yield: 1½ dozen

Scottish Scones

2 cups flour
2 tsp. baking powder
1 tsp. salt
¼ cup butter
2 Tblsp. sugar
¼ cup raisins
2 Tblsp. candied lemon peel
⅔-¾ cup milk

Sift together flour, baking powder and salt. Cut in the butter until mixture resembles coarse meal. Add sugar, raisins and minced peel. Add enough milk to make a soft, but not sticky dough. Handle dough as quickly and lightly as possible. Turn onto a floured board, toss and pat out about 1 inch thick. Cut into triangle or diamond-shaped scones. Place on lightly greased baking sheets and brush with egg or cream. Bake in a 450° oven for about 15 minutes. Serve warm with butter.

Yield: 1½ dozen

Little Tea Cakes

2 cups flour
3 tsp. baking powder
1 tsp. salt
¼ cup butter
¼ cup sugar
½ cup raisins
1 egg
⅓-½ cup milk

Sift the first three ingredients together, make a well and cut in the butter until it resembles coarse meal. Add sugar, raisins, egg and enough milk to make a soft dough. Mix lightly with a few strokes. Handle the dough quickly and as little as possible. Turn out on a floured surface, knead gently ½ minute, roll out ½ inch thick and cut into triangles or diamond-shaped scones. Place on lightly greased sheets, brush with egg or milk, sprinkle with sugar. Bake in a 450° oven for 12-15 minutes.

Yield: 2 dozen

Crumpets

1 pkg. dry yeast
1 cup warm milk
½ cup butter, softened
½ tsp. salt
2 cups flour

Soften yeast in warm milk, let stand 5 minutes; stir well. Add butter, salt and flour. Beat well. Place in a greased bowl, cover let rise in a warm place about 45 minutes, or until doubled in bulk. Stir batter down. Put greased muffin rings on a hot greased griddle. Fill half full. Cook slowly until well risen and browned on the bottom. Turn and brown carefully.

Yield: 1 dozen

Danish Horns

2 pkgs. dry yeast
½ cup warm water
1 Tblsp. sugar
1 cup butter, melted
3¾ cups flour
3 Tblsp. sugar
1 tsp. salt
2 eggs, lightly beaten
cinnamon, sugar, nuts and raisins

Dissolve yeast in warm water, add 1 Tblsp. sugar. Set aside in a warm place until it bubbles. Melt butter and cool. In a large mixing bowl blend together flour, 3 Tblsp. sugar and salt. Make a well, add yeast and butter; mix. Add eggs, blend with wooden spoon until dough forms a ball. Cover and refrigerate overnight. Cut ball into quarters, roll each on sugared surface to size of pie crust. Spread with cinnamon, sugar, nuts and raisins. Cut each quarter into thirds and roll from wide end to point. Pinch sides. Place on *ungreased* cookie sheet, sprinkle with sugar and cinnamon on top, bake in a 325° oven for 20-30 minutes.

Yield: 4 dozen

Prune Kringle

¼ cup milk
2 cups flour
¼ cup sugar
½ tsp. salt
¼ cup butter
2 pkgs. dry yeast
½ cup warm water
1 egg, beaten
1½ cups chopped stewed prunes
3 Tblsp. sugar
3 Tblsp. lemon juice
½ tsp. grated lemon peel

Scald milk; cool to lukewarm. In mixing bowl sift together flour, sugar and salt. Cut in butter with a pastry cutter. Sprinkle dry yeast over warm water, stir until dissolved. Combine lukewarm milk, beaten egg, and yeast with the flour mixture. Stir until well blended. Beat vigorously until it leaves the sides of the bowl. A well-beaten yeast batter looks shiny and smooth. Dough will be quite soft. Cover; let rise in warm place, free from draft, until doubled in bulk, about 45-60 minutes. Combine prunes, sugar, lemon juice and lemon peel. Set aside. Stir dough down and turn out onto *well*-floured surface; divide in half. Roll each half to a 16″x12″ rectangle. Place one half on a greased 15x10-inch jelly-roll pan. Spread with prune mixture. Cover with second half of dough. Seal edges well. Cover; let rise in warm place, free from draft until doubled in bulk, about 30-45 minutes. Bake in a 350° oven about 20 minutes. When cool, glaze with confectioners' sugar frosting, if desired.

Swedish Tea Ring

1 pkg. dry yeast
1/2 cup lukewarm water
1/3 cup butter
1/2 cup boiling water
1/4 cup sugar
1 tsp. salt
1 egg, beaten lightly with fork
3 cups flour
2 Tblsp. melted butter
1/2 cup sugar
2 tsp. cinnamon
1/2 cup raisins, optional

Dissolve yeast in warm water. Set aside. Put 1/3 cup butter in mixing bowl, and pour boiling water over butter, stir with a fork until melted. Add 1/4 cup sugar, salt and egg to butter mixture. Stir in yeast mixture. Add flour, dough will be sticky, an additional 1/2 cup of flour can be added while kneading. Turn onto a lightly floured surface and knead until smooth and elastic. Place in a greased bowl, cover, and let rise in a warm place until double in bulk (1 1/2 hours), punch down. Roll dough into oblong. Spread with melted butter and sprinkle with sugar and cinnamon, which have been combined. Add raisins, if desired. Roll up tightly, beginning at wide end. Seal edges and place sealed edge down on greased baking sheet. Form ring and pinch ends together. Cut 2/3 of the way through ring at 1" intervals. Turn roll on its side. Let rise 35-40 minutes until double in bulk. Bake in a 375° oven for 25-30 minutes. Frost while warm with confectioners' sugar glaze and decorate with nuts and cherries.

Panettone

3 pkgs. dry yeast
1/3 cup warm water
1 tsp. sugar
3/4 cup raisins
1/2 cup citron, diced
2 Tblsp. dark rum
8 egg yolks
1/2 cup sugar
1 tsp. vanilla
1 tsp. salt
grated peel of 1 lemon
1/4 cup melted butter
1 1/2 cups flour

Put yeast, water and 1 tsp. sugar in small bowl. Stir to dissolve yeast. Set aside in a warm place until it bubbles. Combine raisins, citron and rum; set aside. Beat egg yolks, add sugar, beat until pale yellow. Add vanilla, salt and lemon peel. Add yeast mixture and beat. Add butter, a tablespoon at a time; beat well. Add flour and beat 5-10 minutes. Scrape sides of bowl and let dough rest; lightly oil top and cover. Let rise until doubled in bulk, about 1 1/4 hours. Punch dough down, drain raisins and citron and knead them briefly into dough. Put dough into well-greased 7-cup fluted mold, let rise until doubled in bulk, brush with melted butter and bake 10 minutes in a 400° oven, then reduce oven to 325°. Continue baking about 40 minutes, basting often with melted butter. Store in an airtight container.

Yield: 1 loaf

Nut Stollen

1½ pkgs. dry yeast
2 tsp. sugar
⅓ cup warm water
1 cup milk
½ cup sweet butter
1 tsp. salt
2 eggs
2 egg yolks
2 Tblsp. sugar
4½ cups flour
2 Tblsp. sweet butter, melted
2 tsp. grated lemon peel
¼ tsp. cardamom
¼ tsp. ginger
¼ tsp. nutmeg
1 cup golden raisins
1 egg
1 Tblsp. heavy cream
4 Tblsp. sugar
confectioners' sugar icing
½ cup chopped walnuts

Prepare Nut Filling as instructed in recipe below. Dissolve yeast and 2 tsp. sugar in water; let stand until bubbly, about 5 minutes. Heat milk in small saucepan until hot; remove from heat. Stir ½ cup butter and salt into milk; set aside. Beat 2 eggs and the yolks in a large mixing bowl. Gradually beat in 2 Tblsp. sugar until thick and lemon colored. Beat in milk mixture and 2 cups of the flour until smooth. Beat in yeast mixture. Stir in melted butter, lemon peel, cardamom, ginger, nutmeg and remaining flour to form soft dough. Turn dough onto lightly floured surface; knead 5 minutes. Knead in raisins. Let rise covered in large greased bowl in refrigerator overnight. Remove dough from refrigerator; let stand covered 30 minutes. On a lightly floured surface roll dough into 22x12-inch oblong. Spread Nut Filling over dough, leaving 1-inch border on all sides. Mix 1 egg and cream in small bowl. Brush border with part of the egg mixture. Loosely roll up dough beginning at long edge. Pinch seam and ends to seal. Using long sharp knife, cut roll crosswise in half. Transfer pieces to well greased floured baking sheets. Cut second piece lengthwise in half. Working quickly, twist halves together like a braid with sliced edges turned upward. Pinch ends together. Repeat with remaining piece. Let rise until doubled (about 45 minutes). Bake stollen 15 minutes in a 375° oven, brush with half of the egg mixture. Reduce oven to 350° and bake 10 minutes. Brush with remaining egg mixture; sprinkle with 4 Tblsp. sugar. Bake until nut mixture is set, 5 to 10 minutes. (If stollen browns too fast, cover loosely with aluminum foil.) Cool on racks 30 minutes. Drizzle confectioners' sugar icing over stollen, sprinkle with walnuts. Cool completely. Wrap tightly. Refrigerate up to 4 days; serve at room temperature.

Nut Filling:
4 egg whites, at room temperature
2 cups finely chopped walnuts
1½ cups walnuts, ground into meal
1 cup sugar
½ tsp. cinnamon
4 tsp. water

Combine all ingredients except 2 tsp. of the water in medium-size saucepan. Cook, stirring over low heat until warm and sugar dissolves, about 10 minutes; remove from heat. Stir in remaining water. Cool to room temperature. Can be made a day ahead.

Yield: 4 cups

SUZUKI HARUNOBU (Japanese, 1725–1770)
The Maid of Kasamori (Osen); woodblock print
Bigelow Collection

Cakes

Success in creating the perfect cake results from understanding the method of mixing and from following the recipe step by step. *Do not* interchange methods.

Generally there are two types of cakes: those made with shortening (butter cakes) and those made without shortening (sponge cakes).

There are two popular methods for butter cakes. The secret of the conventional method is thoroughly creaming butter and sugar and then beating after the addition of the eggs, which gives a fine and even texture. If the eggs are separated and beaten whites added last, a light, fluffy texture is achieved. The one-bowl, no-creaming method gives a pin-point, velvety texture.

Cakes made without shortening, like sponge or angel-food cakes, are leavened by air that is beaten into the eggs and steam that forms within the cake during baking. Thoroughly beating the eggs is essential for a light, even-grained, springy cake with a slightly pebbled surface. Overbeating the batter after the flour is added will spoil the light texture.

Chiffon cake is an entirely different classification; the result combines the high lightness of an angel-food cake with the tender richness of a butter cake. Egg whites are used as the leavening agent, yet vegetable oil and baking powder are present as well.

The perfect cake is characterized by a light, tender texture, with a delicate, rich flavor and a moist, good keeping quality.

Sherry Zucchini Cake

2 cups grated zucchini
1 tsp. salt
3 cups flour
2 tsp. cinnamon
1½ tsp. soda
½ tsp. salt
1 tsp. baking powder
1 cup vegetable oil
2 cups sugar
3 eggs
2 tsp. vanilla
2 Tblsp. sherry
1 tsp. grated lemon peel
1½ cups chopped nuts
1 cup raisins or chopped dates

Mix zucchini with 1 tsp. salt in colander. Weight down with plate and let drain 1 hour. Squeeze out excess moisture. Sift together flour, cinnamon, soda, salt and baking powder; set aside. Beat together vegetable oil and sugar, add eggs, one at a time, beating well after each addition. Add vanilla, sherry, zucchini and lemon peel; stir to blend. Add dry ingredients, nuts and raisins. Turn into a well-greased 10-inch angel-food cake pan or bundt pan. Bake for 60-75 minutes in a 325° oven. Let stand in pan about 5 minutes, then turn out on rack to cool. If desired, glaze before serving.

Vanilla Glaze:
1½ cups confectioners' sugar
⅛ tsp. salt
1 Tblsp. butter, softened
2 Tblsp. cream or sherry

Mix ingredients together until smooth.

Zucchini Tea Cake

2 cups grated zucchini
1 tsp. salt
1 cup vegetable oil
¾ cup sugar
3 eggs
½ cup honey
2 Tblsp. grated lemon peel
¼ cup fresh lemon juice
2¼ cups flour
2 tsp. soda
½ tsp. baking powder
1½ cups chopped almonds
3 Tblsp. honey

Sprinkle zucchini with salt in colander. Weight with plate and let drain 1 hour. Squeeze out excess moisture. Mix oil, sugar, eggs, ½ cup honey, lemon peel and juice in large mixing bowl. Beat until *thoroughly* blended. Add zucchini, blend well. Sift together flour, soda, baking powder and stir into batter. Fold in nuts. Pour into bundt pan that is well greased and floured. Bake in 350° oven for 45-50 minutes, or until tester comes out clean. Cool on rack for 10 minutes then invert cake and brush with 3 Tblsp. honey. Cool.

Coffee Cookie Cakes

1 cup butter
2 cups brown sugar, packed
2 eggs
3 cups flour
1 tsp. soda
1 tsp. baking powder
¼ tsp. salt
1 tsp. cinnamon
½ tsp. nutmeg
1 cup cold coffee
1 cup raisins

Cream butter and sugar, add eggs one at a time, beating well after each addition. Sift together flour, soda, baking powder, salt and spices. Add alternately with cold coffee. Stir in raisins. Pour batter into a greased 15x10-inch jelly-roll pan, bake 20 minutes in a 350° oven. Leave in pan and ice when cool with a thin confectioners' sugar icing flavored with coffee.

Pumpkin Cake Roll

3 eggs
1 cup sugar
⅔ cup canned pumpkin
1 tsp. lemon juice
¾ cup flour
1 tsp. baking powder
2 tsp. cinnamon
1 tsp. ginger
½ tsp. nutmeg
½ tsp. salt
1 cup finely chopped walnuts

Beat eggs on high speed for 5 minutes. Gradually beat in sugar. Stir in pumpkin and lemon juice. Sift together flour, baking powder, cinnamon, ginger, nutmeg and salt; fold into batter. Line a greased 15x10x1-inch pan with waxed paper and grease the paper. Spread batter evenly in pan. Sprinkle with walnuts. Bake in 375° oven 12-15 minutes, or until tester comes out clean. Turn onto towel that has been sprinkled with confectioners' sugar. Remove paper. Starting at wide end, roll up towel and cake together. Cool. Unroll, spread with filling and roll again.

Cream Cheese Filling:
1 cup confectioners' sugar
6 oz. cream cheese
4 Tblsp. butter
½ tsp. vanilla

Beat sugar with cream cheese, butter and vanilla. Spread over cake. Chill or freeze, wrapped in foil, until ready to use. Cut in slices.

Spiced Pumpkin Cake

2 cups sifted cake flour
2 tsp. baking powder
¾ tsp. salt
1 tsp. ginger
½ tsp. cloves
½ tsp. cinnamon
½ tsp. mace
1½ cups brown sugar, packed
¾ cup canned pumpkin
½ cup butter, softened
2 eggs
¼ cup milk

In a large bowl, sift together dry ingredients. Stir in brown sugar until well mixed. Add pumpkin and butter, with mixer at low, beat mixture for 2 minutes. Beat in eggs and milk. Spread batter evenly into 2 well-greased 8-inch round cake pans, bake in a 375° oven for 30 minutes; or, in a 9-inch tube pan, bake 45-50 minutes or until tester comes out clean. Cool 10 minutes and invert onto racks and cool. Frost with butter-cream icing.

Fresh Apple Cake

2 cups sugar
1 cup vegetable oil
2 eggs
4 cups chopped *unpeeled* apples
3 cups flour
2 tsp. soda
1 tsp. salt
1 tsp. cinnamon
1 cup golden raisins
1 cup dark raisins
1 cup chopped nuts

Mix sugar, oil and eggs until thoroughly blended. Stir in apples, let stand 10 minutes. Sift together flour, soda, salt and cinnamon; stir into apple mixture. Fold in raisins and nuts. Pour into 2 greased 9x5x3-inch loaf pans. Bake in a 350° oven for 60 minutes. Remove from pans and cool on racks.

Carrot Nut Cake

¼ cup orange juice
¼ cup golden raisins, chopped
2 cups flour
1 cup brown sugar, packed
½ cup sugar
2 tsp. soda
¼ tsp. cloves
2 tsp. cinnamon
1 tsp. salt
1 tsp. vanilla
4 eggs
1¼ cups vegetable oil
½ lb. fresh carrots, grated
1 cup walnuts, chopped
1 Tblsp. grated orange peel

In a quart saucepan over medium heat, heat orange juice and raisins to boiling. Reduce to low and simmer uncovered 5 minutes. Set aside. Into a large bowl measure flour, next nine ingredients, and raisin mixture. With mixer at low, beat ingredients just until mixed, constantly scraping bowl. Increase speed to high, beat 4 minutes. Fold in grated carrots, chopped walnuts and orange peel. Pour into a greased 13x9x2-inch pan and bake in a 325° oven for 40-45 minutes, or until tester comes out clean. Cool cake 10 minutes before removing from pan. (Can be made in a greased bundt pan, bake for 55-60 minutes.)

Cream Cheese Frosting:
1 Tblsp. butter
3 oz. cream cheese
1 tsp. vanilla
⅛ tsp. salt
1 cup confectioners' sugar

Cream butter, cream cheese, vanilla and salt until soft. Add confectioners' sugar, working until blended.

Strawberries-and-Cream Cake

1 cup butter
1½ cups sugar
1 tsp. vanilla
¼ tsp. lemon extract
4 eggs
3 cups flour
1 tsp. salt
¾ tsp. cream of tartar
½ tsp. soda
1 cup strawberry jam
½ cup sour cream
½ cup broken nuts

Cream butter, sugar, vanilla and lemon extract until light. Add eggs one at a time, beating well after each addition. Sift together dry ingredients. Combine jam and sour cream; add alternately with dry ingredients to creamed mixture. Stir in nuts. Pour batter into two well-greased and floured 9x5x3-inch loaf pans. Bake for 50 minutes, or until tester comes out clean, in a 350° oven. Cool for 10 minutes before removing cakes. Cool on racks.

Cranberry Cake

2 cups cranberries
1½ cups sugar
2 eggs
1 cup sifted cake flour
4 tsp. baking powder
1 tsp. cinnamon
1 tsp. salt
⅔ cup milk
6 Tblsp. butter, melted
2 tsp. vanilla

Put cranberries in food processor, pulse once or twice to break. Remove and combine with ¼ cup sugar; set aside. Beat eggs, gradually beat in 1 cup sugar, beat until well combined. Sift together flour, baking powder, cinnamon and salt; add to egg mixture alternately with milk. Beat well after each addition. Add butter and vanilla. Beat thoroughly. Fold in cranberries. Pour batter into a well-greased 13x9x2-inch pan. Sprinkle top with ¼ cup sugar. Bake for 25 minutes in a 400° oven.

Pineapple Cake

2 eggs
2 cups sugar
2 cups flour
2 tsp. soda
20-oz. can of crushed pineapple, *undrained*
½ cup chopped pecans
1 tsp. vanilla

Beat eggs until light and fluffy. Add sugar and continue beating until thick. Stir in flour, soda, pineapple, pecans and vanilla; mix thoroughly. Pour batter into greased 13x9x2-inch pan. Bake in a 350° oven until tester inserted in center comes out clean, about 40 to 45 minutes. Let cake cool in pan on rack. This cake uses no shortening.

Cream Cheese Frosting:
2 cups confectioners' sugar
8 oz. cream cheese, softened
¼ cup butter, softened
1 tsp. vanilla
chopped nuts

Combine sugar, cream cheese, butter and vanilla; mix until fluffy. Spread evenly over cooled cake. Sprinkle nuts decoratively over cake. Cut into squares. Serve at room temperature.

ANONYMOUS AMERICAN
Wilson's Albany (strawberries); stencil and watercolor from D. M. Dewey's *Nurseryman's Pocket Book of Specimen Fruit and Flowers*
Gift of Mrs. Alan Tawse

Blueberry Crumb Cake

2 cups flour
1½ cups sugar
¾ cup butter
2 tsp. baking powder
2 egg yolks
1 cup milk
1 tsp. salt
1 tsp. vanilla
2 egg whites, beaten stiff
2 cups fresh blueberries

Blend flour, sugar and butter together with pastry blender or food processor until it resembles coarse meal. Remove 1 cup for topping and set aside. Add the remaining ingredients, except egg whites and blueberries, in order given, to crumb mixture in bowl. Mix until smooth. Fold in stiffly beaten egg whites. Pour into greased and floured 13x9x2-inch pan. Dust the blueberries lightly with flour and spread evenly over batter. Sprinkle reserved crumb topping over the fruit. Bake in a 350° oven about 40 minutes.

Banana Cake

½ cup butter
1¼ cups sugar
3 eggs
1 tsp. lime juice
1½ cups mashed bananas
2 cups flour
2 tsp. baking powder
¼ tsp. soda
¼ tsp. salt
3 Tblsp. milk

Cream butter and sugar slowly, beating well. Add eggs one at a time, beating after each addition. Add lime juice; fold in banana pulp. Sift together remaining dry ingredients and add alternately with milk. Bake in a well-greased bundt pan for 50-60 minutes in a 350° oven. When cool, frost with lemon frosting.

Lemon Frosting:
½ cup butter, softened
1 egg white at room temperature
2 cups confectioners' sugar
2 Tblsp. flour
1 Tblsp. lemon juice

Cream butter until light and fluffy, add egg white and continue creaming. Add remaining ingredients and beat until light and smooth. Spread on cooled cake.

Old-Fashioned Banana Cake

2¼ cups flour
1⅔ cups sugar
1¼ tsp. baking powder
1¼ tsp. soda
1 tsp. salt
4 tsp. vinegar
⅔ cup evaporated milk
⅔ cup butter, softened
3 eggs
1¼ cups mashed ripe bananas

Sift dry ingredients into large mixing bowl and make a well in the center. Add vinegar to evaporated milk. Pour ½ of milk mixture and soft butter into dry ingredients; mix. Add remaining milk, eggs and bananas. Beat at medium speed 2 minutes. Grease well and flour two 9-inch round cake pans. Pour batter into pans. Bake about 40 minutes in a 350° oven. Cool 5 minutes. Turn out on cake racks. Cool completely and frost.

Creamy White Frosting:
½ cup butter, softened
¼ cup evaporated milk
2 tsp. vanilla
4 cups confectioners' sugar

Put butter, milk and vanilla in bowl, add sugar, one cup at a time. Beat until smooth and shiny. Spread between layers and over cake.

Banana-Chip Cake

½ cup butter, softened
¾ cup sugar
2 eggs
1 Tblsp. lemon juice
1 tsp. vanilla
1½ cups flour
2 Tblsp. buttermilk *powder*
¾ tsp. nutmeg
¼ tsp. baking powder
¼ tsp. soda
¼ tsp. salt
¼ cup banana liqueur
¼ cup milk
¼ cup dried banana chips
confectioners' sugar

Cream butter until fluffy. Gradually beat in sugar. Beat in eggs one at a time. Blend in lemon juice and vanilla. Sift together dry ingredients. Add alternately to batter with liqueur and milk, stirring well after each addition. Pour into a 9x5x3-inch greased and floured pan. Chop dried banana chips in processor or blender. Sprinkle on top of batter. Bake in a 350° oven for 55 minutes, or until tester comes out clean. Dust with confectioners' sugar.

Finnish Buttermilk Cake

2½ cups flour
1½ cups sugar
1½ tsp. soda
1 tsp. baking powder
¼ tsp. salt
1 tsp. cinnamon
½ tsp. cloves
1½ cups buttermilk
½ cup melted butter

Sift together flour, sugar, soda, baking powder, salt and spices into a mixing bowl. Stir in buttermilk, mix well. Stir in melted butter and mix well again. Pour into a greased and sugared 9-inch tube pan. Bake in a 350° oven for 1 hour. (This cake has no eggs.)

Chocolate-Chip Cake

1¾ cups boiling water
½ cup butter
1 cup quick oatmeal
1 cup brown sugar, packed
1 cup sugar
2 eggs
1¾ cups flour
1 tsp. soda
½ tsp. salt
1 Tblsp. cocoa
12 oz. chocolate chips
¾ cup walnuts, broken

In a large mixing bowl, pour boiling water over butter and oatmeal. Let stand for 10 minutes. Stir mixture until butter melts. Add sugars and eggs. Mix well. Sift together flour, soda, salt and cocoa; add to batter. Stir in 6 oz. chocolate chips. Pour into a greased 13x9x2-inch pan. Sprinkle walnuts and remaining chips on top. Bake in a 350° oven for 40 minutes.

Caramel Crumb Cake

1¼ cups flour
1 cup brown sugar, packed
½ tsp. salt
5 Tblsp. butter
2 Tblsp. nuts or coconut
1 tsp. baking powder
¼ tsp. soda
½ tsp. cinnamon
1 egg
½ cup buttermilk

Blend flour, sugar and salt. Cut in butter until it resembles fine meal. Measure ¼ cup of this mixture and blend with finely chopped nuts; set aside for topping. Add baking powder, soda and cinnamon to remaining flour mixture, blend. Beat egg well, add buttermilk and stir into flour mixture until all flour is moistened. Pour into a well-greased 8x8x2-inch pan. Sprinkle with crumb mixture. Bake in 375° oven for 25 minutes or until done. Cut into wedges and serve warm or cold.

Bundt Kuchen

1½ cups pecan halves
3 cups sifted cake flour
2 tsp. baking powder
½ tsp. salt
1 cup butter
2 cups sugar
4 eggs, separated
1 cup milk
1 lemon, juice and grated peel
1 tsp. vanilla
2 tsp. whisky (optional)

Grease and flour a bundt pan, place pecan halves in grooves around bottom and sides of pan. Sift together flour, baking powder and salt. Cream butter and gradually add sugar, creaming thoroughly; beat in egg yolks, one at a time, and beat until smooth. Add dry ingredients to creamed mixture alternately with milk; stir in lemon juice and grated peel, vanilla and whisky if desired. Beat egg whites until stiff, buy not dry, then fold in. Carefully spoon batter into nut-lined pan. Bake in 400° oven for 15 minutes, reduce heat to 350° and continue baking 1 hour longer. Cool slightly and turn out of pan.

Oatmeal Cake

1¼ cups boiling water
1 cup quick oatmeal
½ cup butter
1 cup brown sugar, packed
1 cup sugar
2 eggs
1½ cups flour
1 tsp. soda
½ tsp. salt
½ tsp. cinnamon

Pour water over oatmeal and let stand for 20 minutes. Cream together butter and sugars. Add eggs and mix well. Pour oatmeal over creamed mixture and blend. Add dry ingredients, which have been sifted together. Pour into a greased 13x9x2-inch pan. Bake for 30-40 minutes in a 350° oven. Prepare icing and spread on hot cake.

Icing:
6 Tblsp. butter
¾ cup brown sugar, packed
1 tsp. vanilla
1 cup coconut
chopped nuts, if desired

Combine ingredients and mix well. Spread on baked cake and put under broiler until brown.

Three-Layer Pound Cake

6 Tblsp. sugar
3 Tblsp. cocoa
1½ Tblsp. water
½ cup butter, softened
1 cup sugar
2 eggs
1 tsp. vanilla
1½ cups flour
1 tsp. baking powder
¼ tsp. salt
½ cup milk
½ cup chocolate chips
⅛ tsp. soda

Blend sugar and cocoa in heavy small pan. Stir in water. Bring to simmer over low heat, stirring until smooth. Simmer gently 3 minutes; set aside and cool completely. Cream butter until fluffy. Gradually beat in sugar. Beat in eggs one at a time. Blend in vanilla. Sift flour with baking powder and salt. Add dry ingredients to batter alternately with milk, blending well after each addition. Fold in chocolate chips. Pour ⅓ of batter into greased and floured 9x5x3-inch pan. Divide remaining batter in half. Blend half with cocoa mixture and ⅛ tsp. soda. Spoon chocolate mixture over light batter in pan and spread. Top with remaining light batter. Bake in a 350° oven for 65-70 minutes, or until tester comes out clean. Cool in pan 10 minutes. Invert cake onto rack and cool completely.

Almond Pound Cake

Almond Crust:
1/3 cup butter, softened
1/2 cup brown sugar, packed
3/4 cup flour
1 cup chopped almonds

Cream butter with brown sugar until light and fluffy. Add flour and mix until crumbly. Stir in almonds. Pat mixture evenly over bottom and halfway up sides 9x5x3-inch loaf pan. Set aside.

Pound Cake:
1/3 cup butter, softened
3 oz. cream cheese, softened
1/2 cup sugar
2 eggs
2 tsp. vanilla
1 cup flour
1/2 tsp. baking powder
1/4 tsp. salt

Cream butter and cream cheese with sugar until smooth. Blend in eggs and vanilla. Mix in flour, baking powder and salt, which has been sifted together. Spoon batter into crust-lined pan. Bake for 40-45 minutes, or until tester comes out clean, in a 350° oven. Cool on rack. Run knife between cake and pan. Invert cake onto platter. Turn cake top side up. Slice thin.

Chocolate Pound Cake

1 cup boiling water
2 oz. unsweetened chocolate, cut in pieces
2 cups flour
1 tsp. soda
1/4 tsp. salt
1/2 cup butter
1 3/4 cups brown sugar, packed
2 eggs
1 tsp. vanilla
1/2 cup sour cream
confectioners' sugar

Pour boiling water over chocolate; let stand 20 minutes to melt and cool. Sift flour with soda and salt; set aside. Cream butter, sugar, eggs and vanilla until light and fluffy. Add dry ingredients alternately with sour cream, mixing well. Stir in cooled chocolate mixture until combined. Pour into a well-greased 9x5x3-inch loaf pan and bake in a 325° oven for 60-75 minutes, or until tester comes out clean. Cool in pan on rack for 15 minutes. Remove from pan and cool completely on rack. Sprinkle with confectioners' sugar or frost.

Creole Frosting:
12 oz. chocolate chips
1 cup sour cream
1/4 tsp. cinnamon
1 tsp. instant coffee powder
1/4 tsp. salt

Melt chocolate over hot water. Remove from heat. Stir in sour cream, cinnamon, instant coffee and salt. Cool, stirring occasionally, until frosting is thick enough to hold swirls on cake. Frosting stays creamy.

Yogurt Pound Cake

1 cup butter
1 1/2 cups sugar
3 eggs
1 tsp. grated lemon peel
2 1/4 cups flour
1/2 tsp. salt
1/2 tsp. soda
1 tsp. vanilla
1 cup orange *or* peach yogurt

Cream butter and sugar, add eggs and lemon peel; mix well. Sift together flour, salt and soda; add alternately with vanilla and yogurt. Pour batter into a well-greased bundt or tube pan. Bake in a 325° oven 60-70 minutes, or until tester comes out clean.

Breton Bistro Cake

1¼ cups sweet butter, softened
¾ cup sugar
1 egg
2 egg yolks
⅓ cup ground blanched almonds
2 tsp. kirsch
1½ tsp. vanilla
1¾ cups flour
1 egg, lightly beaten
confectioners' sugar
candied violets, optional

Cream butter and sugar until light and fluffy. Beat in 1 egg and the egg yolks, one at a time, beating well after each addition. Beat in almonds, kirsch and vanilla. Fold in flour. Spoon batter into greased 9x1½-inch flan pan with removable bottom; spread evenly. Brush with beaten egg. Bake until top is golden, about 30 minutes in a 350° oven. Cool in pan on rack. Dust lightly with confectioners' sugar; decorate with violets. Texture and flavor improves if allowed to stand covered overnight at room temperature. A crumbly shortbread-like cake.

Parisian Lemon Cake

½ cup butter
1 cup confectioners' sugar
juice and grated peel of 2 lemons
2 extra-large eggs
1 cup flour
2 tsp. baking powder
1 cup confectioners' sugar

Cream butter, sugar and lemon peel until consistency of cream. Add eggs, one at a time and juice of 1½ lemons. Sift together flour and baking powder; fold gently into batter. Bake in a greased 8x8x2-inch pan in a 325° oven for 30-35 minutes, or until tester comes out clean. Cake does not brown. Cool and spread with 1 cup confectioners' sugar mixed with remaining juice of ½ lemon. A very lemony, flat, dense cake.

Lemon Cake

1 cup butter
2 cups sugar
4 eggs
2 Tblsp. grated lemon peel
3 cups flour
2 tsp. baking powder
½ tsp. salt
1 cup milk
fine dry bread crumbs

Cream butter and sugar, beat in eggs, one at a time, add lemon peel. Sift together dry ingredients and fold in alternately with milk. Pour batter into a 9-inch tube pan that has been greased and coated with bread crumbs, bake in a 325° oven for 75 minutes. Remove from oven and invert onto a cake rack; glaze while warm.

Glaze:
⅓ cup lemon juice
¾ cup sugar

Warm the juice and sugar and brush on the bottom and sides of the cake until it is all absorbed.

Rum Cake

1 cup butter
1½ cups sugar
4 eggs
juice & grated peel of 1 lime
1½ cups flour
1 cup cornstarch
2 tsp. baking powder
¼ cup rum

Cream butter and sugar, beat until light and fluffy. Add eggs. one at a time, juice of lime and grated peel. Sift together flour, cornstarch, and baking powder; add alternately with rum. Beat well and pour in greased bundt pan. Bake 60-75 minutes in a 350° oven.

Nut Cake

1 cup butter
2 cups sugar
1 tsp. lemon extract *or*
1½ tsp. vanilla
4 eggs, separated
4 cups sifted cake flour
1 cup milk
½ cup ground walnuts
confectioners' sugar

Cream butter, add sugar and continue beating until light and fluffy. Add flavoring and beaten egg yolks. Add flour alternately with milk. Stir in nuts and gently fold in beaten egg whites. Pour batter into a greased 10-inch tube pan and bake in a 350° oven for 45 minutes, or until a tester comes out clean. Do not open oven during first 40 minutes of baking. Remove from pan, cool and sprinkle top with confectioners' sugar.

Holiday Nut Cake

3½ cups flour
2 tsp. baking powder
½ tsp. salt
¾ cup milk
¼ cup rum *or* brandy
1½ cups butter
2 cups sugar
6 eggs
6 cups chopped pecans or walnuts
sherry
confectioners' sugar

Sift flour, baking powder, salt onto waxed paper; set aside. Combine milk with rum; set aside. Cream butter and sugar until light and fluffy, add eggs, one at a time, beating after each addition. Add flour mixture alternately with milk mixture; blend well. Stir in nuts. Turn batter into lightly greased and floured 10-inch tube pan. Bake in a 275° oven for 2½ hours, or until done. Cool cake in pan 30 minutes on a rack. Remove from pan. Cool completely, wrap in foil. Store in cool place several days to mellow. To serve, sprinkle with sherry and confectioners' sugar. Cut in thin slices and serve at room temperature.

Praline Pecan Cake

7 egg yolks
1½ cups sugar
1 tsp. vanilla
2 cups finely ground pecans
½ cup + 2 Tblsp. flour
1 tsp. baking powder
¼ tsp. salt
⅓ cup melted sweet butter
7 egg whites at room temperature
⅛ tsp. cream of tartar
¼ cup sweet butter
2 Tblsp. heavy cream
¾ cup chopped pecans
pecan halves

Beat egg yolks and ¾ cup of sugar until thick and lemon colored. Beat in vanilla. Combine 2 cups ground nuts, ½ cup flour, baking powder and salt; stir into egg yolk mixture. Stir in melted butter. Beat egg whites and cream of tartar until foamy, gradually beat in ¼ cup of sugar, beat until stiff peaks form. Fold into egg yolk mixture. Pour batter into a 9-inch springform pan that has been greased and floured on the bottom. Bake in a 350° oven 40-45 minutes. Cool on a rack. Mix the remaining ½ cup sugar, 2 Tblsp. flour in a small saucepan; add ¼ cup butter and cream. Heat to boiling; boil, stirring constantly, 1 minute. Remove from heat; stir in ¾ cup chopped pecans. Invert cake onto ovenproof serving dish; remove pan. Spread nut mixture on top of cake. Broil 4 inches from heat until topping bubbles, about 1 minute. Garnish with pecan halves; cool.

ENGLISH (probably London), 1755–1760
Tea caddy; enameled copper with polychrome decorations and tooled gilt-metal mounts
Gift of Rita and Frits Markus

Glazed Nut Cake

2 cups flour
1 tsp. baking powder
1 tsp. soda
⅔ cup chopped walnuts
1 cup butter
1 cup sugar
3 eggs, separated
¾ cup sour cream
2 Tblsp. grated orange peel
2 Tblsp. grated lemon peel
⅛ tsp. salt
dry bread crumbs

Sift together flour, baking powder and soda. Stir a few spoons of dry ingredients into the walnuts. Set aside both mixtures. Cream butter and sugar, beat in the egg yolks, one at a time. Add dry ingredients alternately with sour cream. Add nuts and grated peels. Beat the egg whites with the salt until they hold a peak. Fold into the batter. Pour batter into a 9-inch springform pan that has been greased and dusted with bread crumbs. Bake in a 350° oven for 60 minutes, or until tester comes out clean. Remove cake from oven, prick top quickly and brush hot glaze over the hot cake until absorbed. Let cake cool in the pan.

Glaze:
¾ cup sugar
2 Tblsp. orange juice
2 Tblsp. lemon juice

Mix sugar and juices in small pan and bring to a boil to dissolve sugar.

Marzipan Brandy Cake

⅓ cup sliced almonds
½ cup + 3 Tblsp. butter
⅔ cup sugar
7 oz. almond paste
2 eggs
3 Tblsp. milk
1 Tblsp. brandy
1½ cups flour
1½ tsp. baking powder
¼ tsp. salt
3 Tblsp. sliced almonds

Generously grease 9x5x3-inch loaf pan, sprinkle ⅓ cup almonds evenly on bottom; set aside. Cream softened butter until fluffy. Gradually beat in sugar. Cut almond paste into small pieces and beat in, one piece at a time until mixture is smooth and nearly white, at least 10 minutes. Beat in eggs, one at a time. Blend in milk and brandy. Mix in sifted dry ingredients until incorporated. Turn batter into greased pan. Sprinkle remaining 3 Tblsp. almonds on top. Bake in a 350° oven about 60 minutes, or until tester comes out clean. Cool cake in pan on rack.

Graham Coconut Cake

3 eggs
2¼ cups fine graham cracker crumbs
1½ cups chopped nuts
1½ cups flaked coconut
1 tsp. baking powder
¾ cup sugar
1 cup milk
½ cup butter, melted and cooled

Beat eggs until light and fluffy. Stir in remaining ingredients using wooden spoon. Turn batter into 9x5x3-inch pan that has been greased and floured. Bake in a 250° oven about 1 hour and 35 minutes, or until tester comes out clean. Cool in pan 10 minutes. Invert onto rack and cool completely.

Orange Poppy-Seed Cake

½ cup butter
¾ cup sugar
2 eggs
½ cup sour cream
⅓ cup poppy seeds
¼ cup orange juice
1 Tblsp. grated orange peel
1 tsp. vanilla
1¼ cups flour
½ tsp. baking powder
¼ tsp. soda
pinch salt
confectioners' sugar
poppy seeds

Cream together butter and sugar until fluffy. Beat in eggs, one at a time. Add sour cream, poppy seeds, orange juice, peel and vanilla. Sift together dry ingredients and add to mixture, combining well. Pour batter into a greased and floured 1-quart ring mold and bake in a 350° oven for 40 minutes. Let cake stand for 5 minutes before inverting on cake rack. Cool completely. Sprinkle with confectioners' sugar and poppy seeds.

Pine-Nut Loaves

¾ cup blanched almonds, finely chopped
3 cups flour
4 tsp. baking powder
½ tsp. salt
2 cups heavy cream
2 tsp. vanilla
½ tsp. almond extract
2 cups sugar
4 eggs
¾ cup pine nuts

Grease generously two 9x5x3-inch loaf pans and coat sides and bottom of each pan with the finely chopped almonds. Sift together flour, baking powder and salt; set aside. Whip cream until stiff. Add vanilla, almond extract and sugar. Beat in the eggs one at a time. Carefully fold in sifted dry ingredients. Pour one-quarter of the batter into each pan. Sprinkle each pan with two tablespoons of pine nuts. Cover with remaining batter. Smooth the tops. Sprinkle with remaining nuts. Bake in a 350° oven for 60 minutes, or until tester comes out clean. Remove from oven and brush on glaze. Let cakes cool in pans.

Glaze:
⅓ cup kirsch, warmed
⅓ cup sugar
Mix together, and brush on cakes.

Cocoa Buttermilk Cake

1 cup butter
2 cups sugar
2 eggs, well beaten
3½ cups sifted cake flour
3 Tblsp. + 1 tsp. cocoa
2 tsp. soda
2⅛ cups buttermilk

Cream butter and sugar thoroughly, add eggs and beat well. Sift together flour, cocoa and soda four times. Add dry ingredients alternately with buttermilk, beginning and ending with dry ingredients. Grease and flour bundt pan. Bake in a 325° oven for 60-70 minutes, until tester comes out clean, wait 10 minutes before turning cake out to cool. Can also be baked in two greased and floured 8x8x2-inch layer pans about 40-45 minutes. A light, delicate chocolate cake.

Frosting:
½ cup butter
2 cups confectioners' sugar
6 Tblsp. cocoa
1 tsp. vanilla
½ cup vanilla ice cream, melted

Cream butter and sugar. Add cocoa and vanilla. Add enough melted ice cream to make frosting consistency to spread.

ALBERT ANDRÉ (French, 1869–1954)
Woman at Tea; oil painting, 1917
Bequest of John T. Spaulding

Swiss-Chocolate Sheet Cake

1 cup water
½ cup butter
1½ oz. unsweetened chocolate
2 cups flour
2 cups sugar
2 eggs
1½ cups sour cream
1 tsp. soda
½ tsp. salt

Combine water, butter and chocolate in saucepan; melt and bring to boil. Remove from heat; stir in combined flour and sugar. Add eggs, sour cream, soda and salt; mix well. Pour in a greased 15x10-inch jelly-roll pan. Bake in a 375° oven for 20-25 minutes.

Frosting:
½ cup butter
6 Tblsp. milk
1½ oz. unsweetened chocolate
4½ cups confectioners' sugar
1 tsp. vanilla
½ cup nuts

Frost while warm. Combine butter, milk and chocolate in a saucepan; boil 1 minute. Remove from heat and add confectioners' sugar; beat until smooth. Stir in vanilla. Spread on cake, sprinkle with nuts.

Chocolate Cake

½ cup butter
1 scant cup sugar
4 eggs, separated
1 cup sifted cake flour
1 tsp. baking powder
1 can Hershey's Chocolate Syrup
1 tsp. vanilla

Cream butter, add sugar and egg yolks. Add flour, baking powder, syrup and vanilla. Beat egg whites until stiff, fold into chocolate mixture. Bake in a 350° oven in a well-greased 9-inch springform pan for 50-60 minutes or until tester comes out clean. Cool before removing from pan. Frost with any chocolate frosting, or split in half and frost with sweetened whipped cream flavored with a teaspoon of instant expresso coffee.

Can also be made in a greased and floured 15x10-inch jelly-roll pan. Bake 20-25 minutes.

Icing
¼ cup melted butter
1 tsp. instant coffee powder
1 tsp. cocoa
½ tsp. vanilla
1½ cups sifted confectioners' sugar
2-3 Tblsp. hot milk
¼ cup chopped nuts

Mix ingredients together, adding just enough milk to make it smooth. Ice while warm. Sprinkle with nuts.

White Buttermilk Cake

2 cups sugar
½ cup butter, softened
2 unbeaten egg whites
1¾ cups sifted cake flour
1 tsp. soda
½ tsp. salt
1¾ cups buttermilk
1 tsp. vanilla

Cream together sugar, butter and egg whites. Sift together 2 or 3 times flour, soda and salt. Then combine buttermilk and vanilla. Add dry and liquid ingredients alternately to the creamed mixture, about ⅓ at a time. Pour into two round 9-inch greased pans or a 13x9x2-inch pan. Bake in a 350° oven for 25-30 minutes.

Egg Yolk Frosting:
Beat 2 egg yolks well, add 2 Tblsp. butter and 2 Tblsp. thick cream, 1 tsp. vanilla and sufficient confectioners' sugar to spread.

Hundred-Dollar Chocolate Cake

4 oz. unsweetened chocolate, melted
$\frac{1}{2}$ cup butter
2 cups sugar
2 eggs
2 tsp. vanilla
2 cups flour
2 tsp. baking powder
$\frac{1}{2}$ tsp. salt
$1\frac{1}{2}$ cups milk
1 cup chopped nuts

Melt chocolate in double boiler, set aside. Cream butter and sugar until light and fluffy. Add eggs and vanilla, continue beating. Add chocolate. Sift together dry ingredients and add alternately with milk. Fold in nuts. Pour batter into a greased 10-inch tube pan and bake in a 350° oven for 45 minutes, or until tester comes out clean. Frost when cool.

Frosting:
$1\frac{1}{2}$ oz. unsweetened chocolate
$\frac{1}{4}$ cup butter
$\frac{1}{4}$ tsp. salt
1 egg, beaten
1 Tblsp. vanilla
1 Tblsp. lemon juice
$1\frac{1}{3}$ cups confectioners' sugar
1 cup nuts, chopped

Melt chocolate and butter; set aside. Mix salt, egg, vanilla, lemon juice and confectioners' sugar; add melted chocolate and butter, fold in nuts.

Holiday Fruitcake

4 cups whole pecans
$1\frac{3}{4}$ cups dates, halved
$\frac{3}{4}$ cup candied cherries
$\frac{3}{4}$ cup candied pineapple
1 cup flour
1 cup sugar
$\frac{3}{4}$ tsp. salt
$2\frac{1}{2}$ tsp. baking powder
4 eggs, slightly beaten
1 tsp. vanilla
brandy or orange juice

Combine nuts, dates, coarsely chopped cherries and pineapple in a large bowl. Sift flour, sugar, salt and baking powder together. Add sifted flour to fruit and mix well. Add beaten eggs and vanilla, mix until eggs moisten dry ingredients. Pack firmly in a 10-inch greased angel-food pan with removable bottom. Bake in a 275° oven for $1\frac{3}{4}$ hours. When cool, wrap in orange juice or brandy soaked cloth, then in foil. Store in refrigerator. Will keep several weeks.

Variation: Marzipan-Sealed Fruitcake (omit wrapping in soaked cloth)
2 7-oz. pkgs. almond paste
confectioners' sugar

Shape almond paste into a ball. Lightly dust surface with confectioners' sugar. Roll almond paste into a 16-inch round. Carefully place over cake, gently press to form of cake, smoothing out folds with fingers moistened with water. Trim almond paste even with bottom of cake. Use trimmings to finish off center hole of cake. Wrap cake tightly in foil. Refrigerate up to one month. To serve, slice or if desired, spread butter-cream frosting over marzipan-covered fruitcake.

White Chocolate Cake

¼ lb. white chocolate, melted
1 cup butter
2 cups sugar
4 eggs, separated
1 tsp. vanilla
2½ cups flour
1 tsp. baking powder
1 cup buttermilk
1 cup chopped pecans
1 cup flaked coconut

Melt chocolate over hot water; set aside. Cream butter and sugar, beat in egg yolks, add vanilla and chocolate; mix. Sift together flour and baking powder, add alternately with buttermilk. Beat egg whites until stiff and fold into cake batter. Gently stir in nuts and coconut. Pour into a greased 13x9x2-inch pan and bake for 45 minutes in a 350° oven.

White Chocolate Icing:
2 cups sugar
1 cup butter
1 small can evaporated milk
1 tsp. vanilla

Mix and let stand one hour. Stir occasionally. Cook until soft ball is formed in cold water (235°). Beat until consistency for spreading.

Queen's Cakes

⅓ cup raisins
3 Tblsp. minced candied fruits
2 Tblsp. brandy
½ cup sweet butter, softened
½ cup sugar
2 eggs
¼ tsp. cinnamon
⅛ tsp. nutmeg
⅛ tsp. ginger
1½ cups flour
1 tsp. baking powder
⅛ tsp. salt

Combine raisins, candied fruits and brandy in small bowl; stir to combine. Set aside, stirring occasionally while completing recipe. Lightly grease and flour 36 small muffin tins (1¾ inch). Cream butter and sugar until light and fluffy. Add eggs one at a time, beating well after each addition. Beat in cinnamon, nutmeg and ginger. Stir in fruit-brandy mixture. Sift together flour, baking powder and salt; fold into egg mixture. Spoon batter into prepared tins, filling two-thirds full. Bake in a 350° oven for about 8 minutes until tester comes out clean. Remove from pan and cool on rack. If regular-size muffin tins are used, prepare 18 tins and bake 12-15 minutes.

Yield: 36 tea cakes

Jamaican Rum Fruitcake

1½ cups dark raisins
1½ cups golden raisins
1½ cups currants
1½ cups mixed peel
¾ cup candied cherries, cut
1 cup Jamaica rum
1 cup sherry wine
2 cups flour
1½ tsp. soda
½ tsp. salt
½ tsp. nutmeg
½ tsp. allspice
½ tsp. cinnamon
1 cup sweet butter, softened
1 cup + 2 Tblsp. dark brown sugar, packed
6 eggs
½ cup molasses

Cover fruits with rum and wine, bring to a slow boil, and simmer for 10 minutes; pour into bowl and let macerate overnight. (If time permits, macerate fruit and wine for two months, adding more liquid if needed.) Sift together flour, soda, salt, nutmeg, allspice and cinnamon; set aside. Cream butter, add sugar, beat well. Add eggs, one at a time and beat until light and fluffy. Add molasses. Add dry ingredients and stir just until incorporated. Fold in fruits. Batter will be moist. Pour into a well-greased 13x9x2-inch pan that has been lined on the bottom with waxed paper which had been greased and floured. If desired, two 9x5x3-inch loaf pans can be substituted. Bake in a 350° oven for 1¼ hours, or until a tester comes out clean. Let cake remain in pan for 30 minutes. Turn out on rack and peel off paper. Cool completely and wrap cooled cake in a cheesecloth soaked in rum *or* sherry. Place in an airtight container, or wrap tightly in foil. As cheesecloth dries, drizzle a little rum *or* sherry on to keep it moist. Let ripen for one month before frosting.

Frosting:
1 lb. shelled almonds, ground
1 lb. confectioners' sugar
3 egg whites
1 tsp. almond extract

Mix all ingredients in a food processor or blender. Use wet knife to frost cake.

Variation:
If desired, half the batter may be steamed in a six-cup pudding mold for 3 hours.)

Gingerbread Fruitcake

1 cup raisins
1 cup dried currants
1 cup chopped green candied cherries
1 cup finely chopped walnuts
1 cup blanched whole almonds
1 cup flour
¾ cup sweet butter, softened
2 cups dark brown sugar, packed
2 eggs
2 egg yolks
⅔ cup light molasses
¼ cup brandy
2 tsp. ginger
2 tsp. cinnamon
½ tsp. cloves
½ tsp. nutmeg
2⅔ cups flour
1 cup sour cream
½ cup fresh orange juice
4 tsp. baking powder
corn syrup (optional)

Combine fruits and nuts with 1 cup flour, toss to coat; set aside. Cream butter and sugar until fluffy. Beat in eggs and yolks, one at a time until smooth. Beat in molasses, brandy, ginger, cinnamon, cloves and nutmeg. Stir in 1 cup of flour and sour cream. Stir in orange juice, baking powder and the remaining flour. Beat 1 minute. Stir in reserved fruit mixture. Spoon batter into 2 greased and floured 9x5x3-inch loaf pans. Bake in a 325° oven for 60-75 minutes, or until a tester comes out clean. Cool in pans on racks for 10 minutes. Remove from pans; cool completely on wire rack. Brush tops lightly with corn syrup. Let dry. Refrigerate wrapped in plastic wrap up to 5 weeks.

Egg-Yolk Cake

11 egg yolks
2 cups sugar
½ tsp. salt
2 tsp. vanilla
6 Tblsp. butter
1 cup boiling milk
2 cups sifted cake flour
2 tsp. baking powder

Beat egg yolks until thick and lemon colored. Add sugar gradually, mix in salt and vanilla. Beat thoroughly. Melt butter in boiling milk. Add to egg mixture, beating constantly. Keep stirring while adding boiling milk. Sift together dry ingredients. Quickly beat into egg mixture. Line bottoms of three greased and floured 8-inch round layer pans, bake in a 350° oven for 25-30 minutes. Or use a greased and floured 10-inch tube pan and bake for 60-75 minutes in a 350° oven. Cool on rack for 10 minutes before removing from pans.

Angel-Food Cake (high temp.)

1½ cups egg whites (12)
1 tsp. cream of tartar
½ tsp. salt
1 cup sugar
1 tsp. vanilla
1 cup sifted cake flour
1 cup confectioners' sugar

Before you start, put the angel-food tube pan in the oven, which should be set at 400°. Egg whites should be room temperature. Combine whites with cream of tartar and salt, with an electric mixture, beat until stiff. Slowly fold in granulated sugar and vanilla. Sift together five times the cake flour and confectioners' sugar, fold gently into other mixture. Carefully push batter into *ungreased* 10x4-inch angel-food tube pan. Gently cut through batter with a knife to remove any air pockets. Bake at 425° for 23 minutes. Top will spring back when lightly touched. Invert on funnel until cold. (Yolks may be used in **Egg-Yolk Cake** recipe.)

Basic Sponge Cake

6 eggs, separated
½ tsp. cream of tartar
1½ cups sugar
1 tsp. grated lemon peel
1 tsp. lemon extract
1½ cups sifted cake flour
1 tsp. baking powder
½ tsp. salt
6 Tblsp. cold water

Beat egg whites with cream of tartar until soft peaks form. Set aside. Beat egg yolks for 5 minutes. Gradually add sugar and beat until pale yellow in color. Add lemon peel and extract. Sift together flour, baking powder and salt; add alternately to yolk mixture with water. Fold egg whites into yolk mixture. Pour in an *ungreased* 9-inch tube pan. Bake in 350° oven for 50-60 minutes. Cake is done when pressed lightly with finger; it will spring back. Invert on cake rack. Cool completely before removing from pan. Loosen sides of cake with spatula to release cake from pan.

Passover Sponge Cake

8 eggs, separated
1½ cups sugar
½ cup cake meal
½ cup potato starch
dash of salt
½ cup orange juice
1 tsp. grated orange peel

Beat egg whites until stiff, slowly add 3 Tblsp. sugar, beat thoroughly. Set aside in refrigerator. Beat egg yolks; add remaining sugar, beat until thick and pale yellow in color. Add orange juice and peel, continue beating until fluffy. Sift together cake meal, potato starch and salt, two times. Fold in dry ingredients. Fold egg whites gently into yellow batter. Pour in an *ungreased* angel-food pan. Bake in a 350° oven about 50 minutes or until tester comes out clean. Invert on cake rack. Cool completely before removing from pan. Use a thin metal spatula to release cake from pan.

Nutcake variation:
Substitute 6 Tblsp. cake meal, and 5 Tblsp. potato starch. Fold in 1 cup ground nuts.

Custard Chiffon Cake

¾ cup milk, scalded
8 eggs, separated
2 cups sifted cake flour
1½ cups sugar
1 Tblsp. baking powder
1 tsp. salt
½ cup vegetable oil
2 tsp. vanilla
¼ tsp. cream of tartar

Put milk in saucepan over low heat and heat until scalded. Remove from heat. With a wire whisk, add slightly beaten egg yolks to scalded milk; set aside. Sift together flour, sugar, baking powder and salt. Make a well in the middle, add cooled yolk mixture, oil and vanilla. Beat well. Beat egg whites until foamy, add cream of tartar and beat until stiff, but not dry. Carefully fold egg whites into yolk mixture. Pour into an *ungreased* 10-inch tube pan and bake in a 325° oven for 55 minutes. Invert immediately on a funnel to cool.

Chiffon cakes are versatile and can be baked in many shapes and sizes. Use snap spring-type clothespins on the corners of the pan for legs, invert and cool.

1 oblong pan 13x9x2 inches–bake
45-55 minutes
2 square pans 9x9x2 inches–bake
35-45 minutes
2 loaf pans 9x5x3 inches–bake
45-55 minutes

Brazil-Nut Wine Chiffon Cake

2 cups flour
1½ cups sugar
1 Tblsp. baking powder
1 tsp. salt
1 tsp. cocoa
½ tsp. cinnamon
½ cup vegetable oil
7 egg yolks
½ cup water
¼ cup port wine
1 cup egg whites (7 or 8)
½ tsp. cream of tartar
1 cup Brazil nuts, finely chopped
confectioners' sugar

Sift flour, sugar, baking powder, salt, cocoa and cinnamon in a large bowl. Make a well in the center. Add oil, egg yolks, water and wine. Stir until smooth. Combine egg whites and cream of tartar, beat until very stiff, but not dry. Fold in egg whites just until blended. Fold in nuts. Pour batter into an *ungreased* 10x4-inch tube pan. Bake in a 325° oven for 60-75 minutes or until top springs back when lightly pressed with fingertip. Invert tube pan on a funnel; let stand until cake is thoroughly cooled. Remove from pan. Sprinkle top generously with confectioners' sugar.

Note: See **Custard Chiffon Cake** for variation of pan sizes and baking time.

FRENCH (Vincennes), ca. 1755
Pair of snail-shaped incense burners;
porcelain with ormolu mounts
Forsyth Wickes Collection

Potpourri

This category is a miscellaneous collection of some superb specialties from spicy nuts and crunchy sweets to distinctively tangy beverages and delicate, velvety Madeleines. The main attractions provide delightful variety, create a few surprises, and satisfy the desire for contrast. These are recipes to spark a creative menu and to evoke the graciousness of food shared.

Spiced Nuts

2 cups pecan halves *or* walnut pieces
½ tsp. paprika
½ tsp. cumin
¾ tsp. coarse salt
1 Tblsp. olive oil

Combine ingredients in a large plastic bag. Shake until the spices coat the nuts evenly. Spread nuts onto a baking sheet with edges. Bake in a 400° oven for 5 minutes. Cool completely.

Yield: 2 cups

Cocktail Nuts

4 Tblsp. margarine
1 Tblsp. Worcestershire sauce
1 tsp. Tabasco sauce
1 Tblsp. salad seasoning (Durkee's)
1 tsp. salt
½ tsp. garlic powder
¼ tsp. pepper
1 lb. pecan halves

In a large pan, melt margarine, add remaining ingredients, except nuts. Stir until blended. Add nuts and toss to coat. Cook *covered* over low heat for 20 minutes. Stir occasionally. Drain on brown paper.

Yield: 4½ cups

Sugar-and-Spice Nuts

2 egg whites, lightly beaten
½ cup sugar
2 tsp. cinnamon
1 tsp. cloves
1 lb. pecan halves

Combine egg whites, sugar, cinnamon and cloves; mix well. Add pecan halves and stir until nuts are well coated. Spread on an *ungreased* 15x10-inch jelly-roll pan and bake 20 minutes in a 350° oven.

Yield: 4½ cups

Southern Pecan Dainties

2¼ cups brown sugar
3 cups pecans, chopped
3 egg whites, beaten
¼ tsp. salt
1 tsp. vanilla

Mix above ingredients, drop by scant tablespoon onto greased cookie sheets. Bake in 300° oven about 20 minutes. Cool before removing from cookie sheets.

Yield: 6 dozen

Sour-Cream Candied Walnuts

1½ cups sugar
½ cups sour cream
1½ tsp. vanilla
2-3 cups walnut halves

Heat together sugar and sour cream, stirring constantly until sugar dissolves; continue cooking, stirring frequently, to firm soft-ball stage when tested in cold water (242°). Remove from heat, add vanilla and walnut halves. Stir until creamy. Turn out quickly onto waxed paper and separate nuts, using 2 forks.

Yield: 3 cups

Pistachio Clusters

1 cup pistachio nuts
1 cup sugar
2 Tblsp. sweet butter, cut in bits
1 tsp. vanilla

Combine nuts, sugar and butter, heat over moderately high heat, stirring until sugar begins to melt. Cook, stirring constantly, for 3 minutes, or until the sugar is light brown caramel, remove from heat and stir in the vanilla. Working quickly, with 2 teaspoons drop rounded teaspoons of the mixture onto a lightly buttered baking sheet, let the clusters stand at room temperature until they are hardened, and store them in an airtight container lined with waxed paper. Keep in a cool dry place.

Yield: 3½ dozen

Sour-Cream Pralines

4 cups sugar
2 cups sour cream
¾ tsp. salt
3 cups pecans, chopped coarse

Carmelize 2 cups sugar in a heavy pan, over very low heat, stirring constantly while sugar is melting. Cook until sugar is a golden brown. Make a syrup with cream, salt and remaining sugar; pour carefully into the caramelized sugar all at one time, stirring rapidly until it begins to boil. Then boil without stirring to a soft-ball stage (238°). Pour into a shallow pan to cool. Beat until creamy and then add nuts. Drop by teaspoonfuls on waxed paper.

Yield: 3-4 cups

Strawberry Chews

1 lb. coconut
⅔ cup almonds
1 can sweetened condensed milk
½ tsp. vanilla
1 Tblsp. sugar
3 3-oz. pkgs. strawberry Jello
few drops red food coloring
confectioners' sugar frosting, tinted green

Grind coconut and almonds in blender until fine. Add milk, vanilla, sugar, 1½ pkgs. Jello and red food coloring. Mix well. Shape into berries, roll in remaining Jello. Add stems and leaves with green frosting. Store in airtight container or in freezer.

Yield: 1½ dozen

Chocolate-Covered Strawberries

3-4 pts. fresh whole strawberries
5 oz. semi-sweet chocolate
5 Tblsp. sweet butter
3 Tblsp. light Karo syrup
1 Tblsp. Grand Marnier *or* 1 Tblsp. coffee *or* 1 tsp. vanilla

Rinse strawberries with cold water, but do not remove stems; pat dry thoroughly with paper towels. Set aside. Combine chocolate, butter and syrup in pan over low heat. Do not boil. When melted, blend with wooden spoon and add flavoring of your choice. Strawberries should be at room temperature for dipping. Dip strawberries into chocolate, one at a time, keeping stem away from chocolate. Gently shake off excess chocolate. Put strawberries on aluminum foil to set, about 10 minutes. Best served the same day.

Coconut Chips

1 medium coconut
½ tsp. salt

Puncture eyes of coconut with ice pick or nail; reserve coconut water for other use. Bake coconut 15 minutes; remove from oven. Tap coconut shell with hammer to open; remove from shell. Pare brown skin from coconut; cut into 2″-long paper-thin slices. Place in single layer on a large baking sheet; sprinkle with salt. Bake in a 350° oven, stirring occasionally, until golden brown and crisp. Serve warm or at room temperature.

Yield: 2½ cups

English Toffee Candy

1 cup butter
1 cup sugar
2½ oz. slivered almonds
6 oz. chocolate chips
1 cup chopped walnuts (optional)

Melt butter. Add sugar gradually, then almonds, stirring constantly until mixture reaches the hard-ball stage (265°). Spread on large greased cookie sheet. Add chocolate chips and spread until melted. If desired, sprinkle walnuts on top. Refrigerate until hard.

Cheese Wafers

1 cup butter
2 cups flour
2 cups sharp cheese, grated
¼-½ tsp. cayenne pepper
½ tsp. salt
2 cups Rice Krispies

Cut butter into flour. Blend in cheese, cayenne, salt; stir with cereal. Roll into marble-size balls. Press with fork and place on *ungreased* cookie sheet. Bake in a 350° oven for 10-15 minutes.

Yield: 5 dozen

Caraway Cheese Straws

½ cup butter
4 oz. cream cheese
1 cup flour
¼ tsp. salt
1 egg yolk
2 tsp. milk
½ cup grated parmesan cheese
2 tsp. caraway seeds

Cream butter and cream cheese, blend flour and salt gradually. Form into ball. Chill. Divide dough in half. Roll each half into a rectangle, ½″ thick. Dilute egg yolk with milk and brush on pastry. Sprinkle with grated parmesan cheese and caraway seeds. Roll lightly with rolling pin. Cut pastry into strips ¾x3″. Place on greased cookie sheet. Bake on upper shelf at 450° for 8-9 minutes. Serve warm.

Cheese Cookies

1 lb. extra-sharp cheese, grated
1 cup margarine
¼ tsp. hot pepper flakes
2 cups flour
7 oz. Special K cereal

Cream cheese and margarine; add pepper flakes and flour. Stir in cereal. Roll into small balls, flatten with fork. If desired place 1 pepper flake in center of each cookie. Place on *ungreased* cookie sheets and bake in a 325° oven for 30-35 minutes.

Yield: 6 dozen

Savory Cheese Wafers

½ lb. brie *or* roquefort
½ cup butter
1¼ cups flour
2 tsp. dry mustard
½ tsp. salt
white pepper
1 egg, beaten with ½ tsp. water
1 cup chopped walnuts

Scrape the powdery white off the crust of the cheese and cut away any tough parts of the crust. Cut cheese and butter into small pieces, place in food processor along with flour, dry mustard, salt and white pepper. Process for a few seconds until dough is formed. Form dough into two rolls about 1½″ in diameter. Turn the rolls in the beaten egg. Dry them for a few minutes, then roll in chopped walnuts. Wrap and chill rolls. Cut each roll into 15 slices and bake on *ungreased* cookie sheet for 12-15 minutes in a 425° oven.

Yield: 2½ dozen

Soufflé Crackers

saltine crackers
melted butter
ice water

Float saltine crackers in ice water until well soaked, but not to the breaking point. Place soaked crackers in a pan brushed with butter. Tilt pan and drain off excess water and then brush melted butter on top of crackers. Place in a 400° oven for 15 minutes, then reduce the heat to 300° and continue baking until a deep golden brown, approximately 45 minutes. When cooled, store in an airtight container.

Golden Cheddar Puffs

1 cup water
½ cup butter
¼ tsp. salt
1 cup flour
4 eggs
¾ cup shredded sharp Cheddar
1-2 Tblsp. seasame seeds

Heat water, butter and salt in medium saucepan to boiling; with wooden spoon stir in flour. Cook, stirring constantly, until paste is smooth and almost cleans side of pan; remove from heat. Add eggs one at a time, beating well with spoon after each addition. Beat in ½ cup of cheese. Drop tablespoons of dough 1 inch apart onto greased baking sheets. Sprinkle with remaining cheese and sesame seeds. Bake in a 375° oven until puffs are firm and golden brown, 25-35 minutes. Pierce top of each puff with sharp knife. Bake 5 minutes. Serve warm.

Yield: 4 dozen

Baby Popovers

vegetable oil
6 eggs
1½ cups flour
1 tsp. salt
½ tsp. pepper
pinch nutmeg
2 cups milk
½ cup heavy cream
jam of choice

Preheat oven to 400° and heat small muffin tins, brushed with vegetable oil. In a blender put eggs, flour, salt, pepper and nutmeg; blend. With motor running slowly add milk and cream. Fill cups ½ full, add ½ tsp. jam, pour in remaining batter to ⅔ full, bake 40-50 minutes.

Yield: 1½ dozen

WALTER CRANE (British, 1845–1919)
When the Pie is Open; color wood engraving from *Sing a Song of Sixpence*
Anonymous Gift

Lemon Chess Southern Pie

1½ cups sugar
4 tsp. cornstarch
2 tsp. grated lemon peel
4 eggs
½ cup fresh lemon juice
5 Tblsp. sweet butter, melted and cooled
1 9-inch pie shell

Sift sugar and cornstarch together into a large bowl. Stir in lemon peel. Beat in eggs, one at a time. Gradually stir in lemon juice. Add butter, blend well. Partially bake pie shell for 5 minutes. Pour filling into pie shell. Bake in a 325° oven for 45-55 minutes, until golden brown and puffed. Cool to room temperature before serving. Filling will thicken and set to a rich, sweet cheese-like texture.

Shoofly Pie

¾ cup flour
½ cup brown sugar, packed
½ tsp. cinnamon
⅛ tsp. cloves
⅛ tsp. ginger
⅛ tsp. nutmeg
¼ tsp. salt
2 Tblsp. butter
½ cup molasses
¾ cup boiling water
1½ tsp. soda
1 egg yolk, well beaten
9-inch pie shell

Mix together the first seven ingredients. Cut in the butter with pastry blender until mixture is crumbly. Set aside. Combine molasses, water, soda and egg yolk. Alternate layers of crumbs and liquid mixture in the pie shell, ending with crumbs. Bake in a 450° oven for 10 minutes. Reduce heat to 350°, bake about 20 minutes longer or until firm.

Ladyfingers

3 eggs, separated
⅓ cup confectioners' sugar
½ tsp. vanilla
½ cup sifted cake flour
⅛ tsp. salt
⅓ cup confectioners' sugar

Beat egg whites until stiff, gradually beat in ⅓ cup confectioners' sugar. Set aside. Beat egg yolks until thick and light colored, fold in vanilla and thrice-sifted flour, sugar and salt. *Carefully fold* dry ingredients into egg whites three tablespoons at a time; do not overmix. Drop batter from spoon on an *ungreased* paper-lined baking sheet. Dust with confectioners' sugar and bake in a 350° oven for 10 minutes. Serve plain or put together in pairs with whipped cream, custard filling, lemon curd, or softened cream cheese mixed with chopped candied ginger.

Scotch Shortbread

1½ cups sifted cake flour
¼ cup cornstarch
½ cup butter
⅓ cup sugar

Sift cake flour and cornstarch together. Cream butter, gradually add sugar and beat until light and fluffy. Add dry ingredients gradually until dough is stiff enough to work with hands. Knead in remaining dry ingredients until well blended and dough forms a ball. Shape into two round cakes (4 inches) on a cookie sheet. Score almost through with knife and prick with a fork. Edges may be fluted or pressed with tines of fork, if desired. Bake in a 325° oven for 15 minutes, reduce heat to 275° and continue baking for 30 minutes. Sprinkle with sugar (if desired) and let cool for 5 minutes before removing from cookie sheet. When thoroughly cool store in airtight container.

Cream Puffs

Use recipe for eclairs.
Drop dough by spoonfuls on a cookie sheet, 2 inches apart. Use tablespoon for large puffs, and a teaspoon for small ones. Bake until there are no beads of moisture on the puffs, about 40 minutes for large puffs. When cool, split and fill with desired filling.

Yield: 16 large, 32 small, 50 petite

Lemon Curd

2 tsp. cornstarch
¼ cup fresh lemon juice
6 Tblsp. sugar
3 Tblsp. sweet butter, cubed
3 egg yolks
2 tsp. grated lemon peel
1 egg

Dissolve cornstarch in lemon juice. Combine remaining ingredients in heavy saucepan. Whisk in lemon juice mixture. Set over medium heat and whisk until thickened and smooth, about 5 minutes. Refrigerate in a small bowl. Cover surface with waxed paper to prevent skin from forming. Lemon Curd can be prepared 1-2 days ahead.

For ladyfingers:
Spread 2 tsp. lemon curd on flat side of one ladyfinger, press flat surface of another ladyfinger on curd to form sandwich.

For small cream puffs:
Split puffs in half and fill with small amount of lemon curd.

Madeleines

4 eggs
1½ cups sugar
1 tsp. grated lemon peel
1 tsp. vanilla
2 cups flour
¾ cup clarified butter

Combine eggs, sugar and peel; heat over warm water until batter is warm. Remove from heat, beat until light and fluffy and tripled in bulk. Add vanilla. Fold in flour and then butter. Fill well-greased madeleine molds ⅔ full. Bake until golden, 10 minutes in a 450° oven. Remove from tins as soon as baked. Regrease molds before second baking.

Yield: 4 dozen

Madeleines II

4 eggs, separated
½ cup sugar
1 Tblsp. lemon juice
1 tsp. grated lemon peel
¾ cup flour
½ cup butter, melted and cooled

Beat egg yolks and sugar until thick and forms a ribbon when dropped from spoon. Add lemon juice and peel. In separate bowl, beat egg whites with a pinch of salt until stiff. Fold in ¼ of whites to yolk mixture. Pour yolk mixture over balance of egg whites. Fold. Add flour and fold it in. Add melted butter and carefully fold into mixture. Fill greased molds ⅔ full. Bake on low rack of a 400° oven for 15-20 minutes. Remove from tins as soon as baked. Regrease molds before second baking.

Yield: 4 dozen

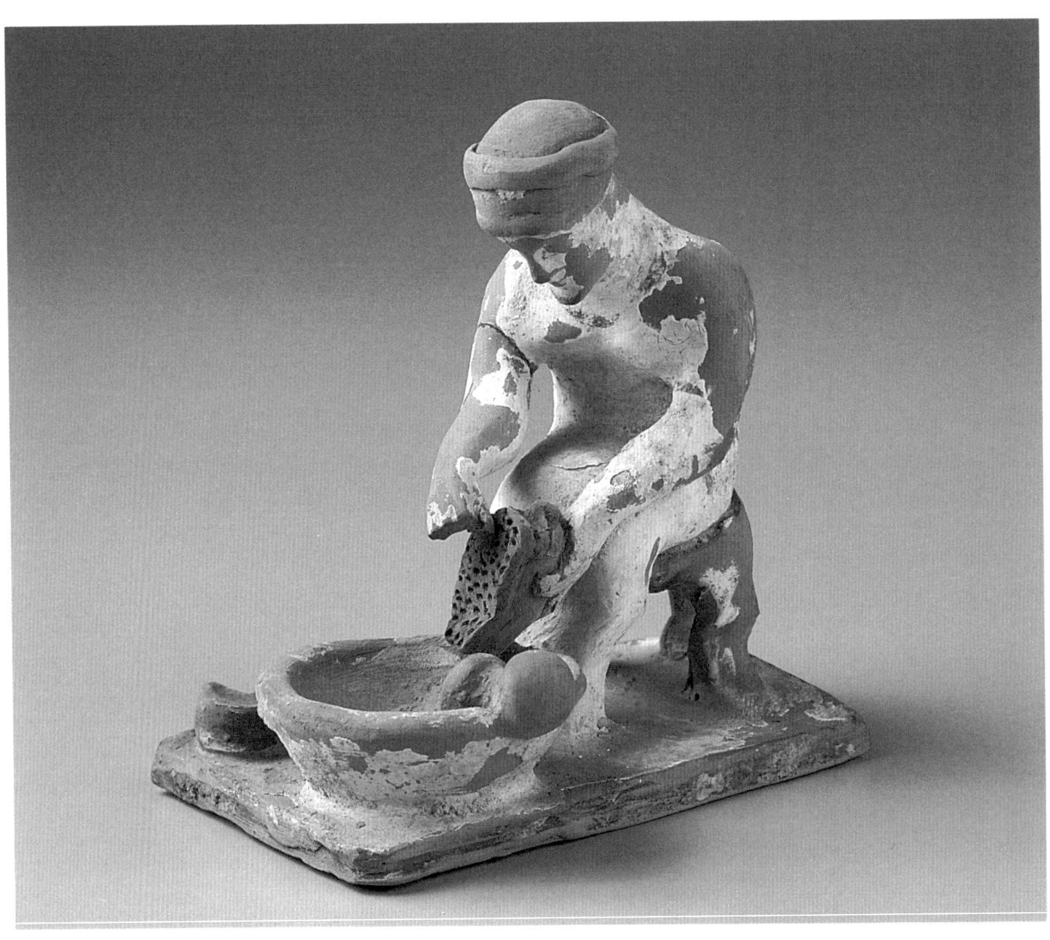

BOEOTIAN (Tanagra), 5th century B.C.
Woman grating cheese; terracotta
Catherine Page Perkins Fund

Chocolate Eclairs

1 cup water or milk
½ cup butter
⅛ tsp. salt
1 cup flour
4 eggs

Boil water or milk, butter and salt; add flour all at once, stirring constantly with wooden spoon until paste leaves sides of pan and forms a smooth ball. The eggs which are then beaten in, act as a leavening agent, causing the puffs to rise to several times their original size during baking. Cooked mixture must be removed from heat and cooled slightly before eggs are added. If paste is too hot, eggs will coagulate and prevent dough from puffing in oven. If past is cooled too long, eggs will not easily blend in and dough will be lumpy. Place in mixing bowl and add eggs, one at a time, beating thoroughly after each addition. Beat batter until thick and shiny; it should break off when spoon is raised. Using a pastry bag, make strips 1x4½″ for large eclairs and ½x2″ for small. Place on a lightly greased cookie sheet and bake in a 425° oven for 15 minutes; then, heat reduced to 350°, 15 to 20 minutes longer. Prick with sharp knife to let out steam. Turn off oven and allow large puffs to remain 15 minutes, small puffs 10 minutes. Bake until there are no beads of moisture on puffs. Small puffs require less baking time. When cool, split and fill with whipped cream or custard filling. Frost tops with chocolate icing.

Yield: 12 large, 24 small

Tomato Bouillon

5½ quarts boiling water
20 beef bouillon cubes
4 46-oz. cans tomato juice
1½ cups sugar
4 sticks cinnamon
3 Tblsp. whole cloves

Combine ingredients and simmer about 1 hour.

Yield: 55 cups

Iced Tea

6-oz. can frozen lemonade
3 sprigs mint
½ cup sugar (scant)
11 tea bags
3 qt. + 1 cup boiling water

Pour boiling water over first 4 ingredients. Let steep 5 minutes. Remove tea bags and refrigerate.

Yield: 14 cups

Tea Sandwiches

A feast for the palate as well as the eye, tea sandwiches are always dainty, attractive and festive. Choose garnishes that enhance the flavor of the filling, so sandwiches will taste as good as they look.

For tea sandwiches use thinly sliced bread of firm texture. It is best to use day-old bread unless the sandwiches are to be rolled. Fresh bread is used for rolled pinwheel sandwiches. Bread should be carefully sliced with a long, sharp knife, preferably a serrated blade.

To prevent fillings from soaking into bread, cream softened butter until light and fluffy. Spread a very thin layer of butter over prepared bread slices before adding the filling.

Sandwich fillings are spread evenly and to the very edge of the bread. Most fillings can be made a day ahead and stored in the refrigerator. Fillings made of uncooked vegetables should be prepared just before serving to avoid loss of vegetable juices and crispness.

If a large quantity of sandwiches is made, set up an assembly line for each step—cutting, spreading, garnishing, and storing.

Sandwiches prepared ahead can be stored in the refrigerator wrapped in plastic wrap or placed in a pan lined with a damp cloth and covered. Many sandwich ingredients are suitable for freezing for a period of 2-3 weeks. Those that *do not* freeze well include egg whites (they become rubbery), vegetables and fruits (they lose crispness), and mayonnaise.

Fancy Sandwiches

Canapes

These open-face sandwiches are best assembled just before serving; otherwise they become soggy. Beautiful canapes begin with clever cutting of assorted breads. First remove all crusts and cut into fancy shapes—crescents, rounds, stars, diamonds, etc.—with cookie cutters. Prepare bread early in the day, wrap tightly, and store at room temperature. Prepare fillings of contrasting flavors, textures, and colors ahead of time and refrigerate, but bring spreads to room temperature before using so bread does not tear. Decorate with edible garnishes like chopped parsley, sliced olives, ground nuts, sieved hard-boiled egg yolks, grated cheeses, thinly sliced vegetables or fruits, capers, and caviar.

Closed Sandwiches

Cut the crust from bread with a sharp knife. To make full-size sandwiches, spread one side of each buttered slice lightly with filling, spreading evenly to the edges. Cover with the other slice, and press gently together. Wrap each sandwich in plastic wrap and chill at least 1 hour before cutting into small sandwiches. Cut each full-size sandwich into 4 squares, 4 triangles, *or* 4 strips. Garnish by dipping an edge in mayonnaise or softened butter and then into minced fresh herbs.

Pinwheel Sandwiches

Using very fresh bread, remove crusts from six (or more) slices. Place slices between waxed paper and gently run a rolling pin over bread to increase flexibility. Select fillings for rolled sandwiches that will hold them together. Smooth butter or cream-cheese mixtures are especially good. Do not attempt to use salad mixtures for this type of sandwich.

PETER PLAMONDON (American, b. 1939)
Quilt with Green Teapot; oil painting, 1975
Gift of Stephen and Sybil Stone

First, spread one side of each slice lightly with softened butter, then cover with a generous amount of filling, leaving 1/4-inch border on all sides. Start at one end of the slice and roll up tightly as a jelly roll. Wrap each roll in plastic wrap and chill for at least one hour. Cut in 3/8-inch slices across rolls and serve.

If a garnish is desired, place a row of selected food end to end, along starting edge of roll, which places the garnish in the center of the pinwheel. Depending on filling, select an appropriate garnish—stuffed olives, small sweet pickles, fresh or canned asparagus spears, cherries, *or* nasturtiums.

Ribbon Sandwiches

Remove crusts from two thin slices of dark bread and two thin slices of white bread; trim as necessary, making all slices the same size. Spread one side of each slice lightly with softened butter. Cover *three* slices with filling (or use various flavored fillings), spreading evenly to edges of bread. Stack slices like a layer cake, alternating white and dark slices, top with fourth slice of bread, buttered side down. Press layers together lightly to make a compact stack. Wrap with plastic wrap and refrigerate for at least one hour. Slice the stack into six ribbon sandwiches. Cut each ribbon into thirds for a total of 18 finger-size sandwiches.

Like pinwheel sandwiches, the filling should be of the type that will become firm when chilled in order to hold the pieces of bread together.

Butters

Shrimp Butter

1 cup butter, softened
1 cup cooked shrimp, minced
1/4 tsp. salt
1/8 tsp. paprika
1 Tblsp. lemon juice

Cream butter thoroughly. Add shrimp, salt, paprika and lemon juice; mix together. Use as a sandwich filling or canape spread.

Watercress-Butter Roll-ups

watercress, rinsed and dried
1/4 cup butter, softened
1 tsp. grated onion
pinch salt

Follow directions for pinwheel sandwiches. Coarsely chop watercress; set aside. Cream butter thoroughly, add onion and salt. Spread on prepared bread slices. Place watercress over buttered bread, letting the green leaves protrude. Roll each slice like a jelly roll. Wrap each roll in plastic wrap and chill. Cut into slices across roll. Serve.

Seasoned Butter

1/2 cup butter, softened
1/4 tsp. pepper
1 tsp. chili powder *or*
1 tsp. paprika *or*
1 tsp. curry powder *or*
1 tsp. dill weed

Cream butter thoroughly. Add pepper and one suggested seasoning and blend until smooth. Spread on toast rounds or use for sandwich filling.

Poppy-Seed Butter

1/2 cup butter, softened
1/2 cup poppy seeds

Cream butter thoroughly. Add poppy seeds and blend together. Spread on bread rounds. Serve cold or place rounds under broiler until hot and bubbly.

Savory Butter Pinwheels

¼ cup butter
½ cup grated sharp cheese
1 Tblsp. mayonnaise
2 Tblsp. chopped parsley
1 tsp. prepared mustard
1 tsp. Worcestershire sauce

Follow directions for pinwheel sandwiches. Combine softened butter with the other ingredients. Spread on prepared bread slices. Roll each slice like a jelly roll. Wrap each roll in plastic wrap and chill. Cut into thin slices across roll and toast under broiler.

Chive Butter

½ cup butter, softened
4 drops Worcestershire sauce
2 Tblsp. chopped chives *or*
2 Tblsp. chopped sweet onion

Cream butter thoroughly. Add Worcestershire sauce and chopped chives *or* sweet onion. Spread on bread rounds. Serve cold or place under broiler until hot and bubbly.

Olive Butter

½ cup butter softened
½ tsp. lemon juice
3 Tblsp. chopped olives

Cream butter thoroughly. Combine lemon juice and chopped olives with butter. Spread on bread rounds or use for sandwich filling.

Ginger Butter

16 thin slices whole-wheat bread
½ cup butter, softened
2 Tblsp. minced preserved ginger

Trim crusts from whole wheat bread. Cream butter thoroughly. Add minced ginger, blend. Spread about 1 Tblsp. ginger butter on 8 bread slices; top each with an unbuttered bread slice. Place sandwiches on damp paper-towel-lined jelly-roll pan. Cover sandwiches with damp paper towels and plastic wrap. Refrigerate until ready to serve. Cut each sandwich diagonally into quarters.

Cinnamon-Butter Pinwheels

12 slices very fresh white bread
¼ cup sugar
2 tsp. cinnamon
⅓ cup butter, softened

Follow direction for Pinwheel Sandwiches. Combine sugar and cinnamon; set aside. Cream butter thoroughly. Add cinnamon sugar to butter and beat until light and fluffy. Spread on prepared bread slices. Roll each slice like a jelly roll. Wrap each roll in plastic wrap and freeze or wrap in a damp cloth and chill. Cut into thin slices across roll. Serve plain or toast lightly under broiler.

Lemon Butter

½ cup butter, softened
1½ Tblsp. lemon juice
Grated peel of 1 lemon

Cream butter thoroughly. Add lemon juice and peel, blend well. Use as spread or filling.

Orange Butter

1 cup butter, softened
1 tsp. grated orange peel
¼ cup orange juice
¼ cup brown sugar, packed

Cream butter thoroughly. Combine all ingredients and beat until well blended.

Spiced-Pear Butter

¾ cup sweet butter, softened
1 very ripe pear, unpeeled, cored, cut into 1-inch pieces
2 Tblsp. honey
1 tsp. lemon juice
½ tsp. cinnamon
¼ tsp. grated lemon peel
⅛ tsp. nutmeg

Cream butter in processor, add pear, small amount at a time, process until smooth. Add remaining ingredients and process until well blended. Spread on bread rounds, or serve with muffins, scones or toast.

SOUTHERN ITALIAN (Campania), 4th century B.C.
Fish plate; terracotta
Henry Lillie Pierce Fund

Cream-Cheese Spreads

Pineapple-Cheese Wafers

3 oz. cream cheese
3 Tblsp. mayonnaise
½ cup chopped pecans
½ cup crushed canned pineapple, drained

Blend softened cream cheese with mayonnaise. Add pecans and crushed pineapple. Spread on crisp crackers or whole-wheat bread rounds.

Raspberry Dainties

3 oz. cream cheese
1-2 tsp. cream
½ cup raspberry jam
¼ cup toasted coconut

Cut bread into fancy shapes. Combine softened cream cheese with enough cream until consistency to spread on bread. Spread jam on top of cream cheese and sprinkle with toasted coconut.

Cream-Cheese-and-Strawberry Sandwiches

½ tsp. vanilla
1 tsp. sugar
8 oz. cream cheese, softened
milk
1 loaf thin-sliced white bread
fresh strawberries

Add vanilla and sugar to softened cream cheese, slowly add enough milk until consistency to spread. Remove crusts and spread cream cheese on each slice. Cut into quarters. Freeze. Shortly before time to serve, remove from freezer and place sliced strawberries on top. Peaches can be substituted.

Ginger Sandwiches

1 Tblsp. cream
8 oz. cream cheese, softened
2 Tblsp. preserved ginger, finely chopped

Add cream to cream cheese until consistency to spread. Blend in chopped ginger. Spread on date-nut bread.

Nut Spread

6 oz. cream cheese
2-3 tsp. milk
⅓ cup minced nuts (walnuts, pecans *or* pistachios)

Combine softened cream cheese with enough milk until consistency for spreading. Add nuts, blend well.

Pimento-Walnut Sandwiches

3 oz. cream cheese, softened
½ cup mayonnaise
½ cup chopped walnuts
½ cup chopped pimentos
⅛ tsp. salt

Combine softened cream cheese with mayonnaise. Add walnuts, pimento and salt; mix. Spread on brown or nut bread.

Salmon-Dill Rounds

pumpernickel bread
3 oz. cream cheese, softened
2 tsp. milk
1 tsp. minced fresh dill *or* ¼ tsp. dried dill weed
2 oz. smoked salmon, chopped

Using biscuit cutter, cut 24 bread rounds. Combine softened cream cheese with milk and dill until blended. Spread each bread round with a teaspoonful of the cream cheese mixture. Top each round with ½ teaspoonful chopped salmon. Place sandwiches on damp, paper-towel-lined pan. Cover with plastic wrap and refrigerate until ready to serve.

Watercress Canapes

4 oz. cream cheese, softened
1 tsp. horseradish
⅛ tsp. salt
2 bunches watercress, rinsed, dried, finely chopped

Beat softened cream cheese until smooth. Add horseradish and salt. Stir in watercress. Spread on canape shapes.

Date-Bacon Sandwiches

4 oz. cream cheese, softened
1/3 cup pitted dates, chopped fine
5 slices bacon, cooked crisp, drained and crumbled
12 slices pumpernickel bread

Cream the cheese, mix in dates and bacon until combined. Remove crusts from bread, spread mixture on 6 slices, top with remaining slices, press together gently. Quarter each sandwich diagonally.

Roquefort Spread

3 oz. cream cheese, softened
2 oz. Roquefort cheese
1-2 Tblsp. brandy *or* sherry

Combine softened cheeses and add enough liquid to give consistency for spreading.

Mayonnaise Fillings

Bacon Filling

7 slices crisp bacon, chopped
1 pimento, chopped
1/4 cup mayonnaise

Combine all ingredients. Use as a spread or sandwich filling.

Ham Filling

1 cup ground cooked ham
1 1/2 tsp. minced onion
1/2 tsp. dry mustard
2 Tblsp. mayonnaise

Combine all ingredients. Use as a spread or sandwich filling.

Ham-Salad Filling

1 cup ground cooked ham
1 hard-boiled egg, chopped
3 sweet pickles, chopped
1 oz. pimento, chopped
1 Tblsp. green pepper, chopped
1 Tblsp. sugar
2 Tblsp. vinegar
1/3 cup mayonnaise

Combine the ground ham with finely chopped egg, pickles, pimento and green pepper; set aside. Combine sugar, vinegar and mayonnaise, blend well. Mix with chopped ingredients.

Crabmeat Filling

6 oz. crabmeat
2 Tblsp. celery, finely chopped
1 tsp. curry powder
mayonnaise

Shred crab meat and discard all tough spines. Mix crabmeat, celery and curry powder with enough mayonnaise to moisten.

Chicken-Nut Filling

1 cup chopped, cooked white meat of chicken
1/4 cup minced celery
1/4 cup chopped almonds
1/4 cup mayonnaise
1/2 tsp. salt
dash pepper

Combine all ingredients together. Spread as sandwich filling.

Watercress-Ham Filling

8 thin slices white bread
butter, softened
1/2 cup minced watercress
1/4 cup minced ham
2 Tblsp. mayonnaise

Follow directions for Ribbon Sandwiches. Trim crusts from bread. Spread one side of each slice with butter. Combine watercress, ham and mayonnaise; spread mixture on 6 buttered slices. Stack 3 slices, watercress side up, top with a bread slice, buttered side down. Repeat to make second stack. Wrap each stack separately with plastic wrap. Refrigerate for at least one hour. To serve, cut each stack into 6 slices, then cut each slice crosswise in half.

Broccoli Tea Sandwiches

1 loaf thin-sliced whole-wheat bread
1 cup mayonnaise
2 cups fresh broccoli flowerettes
onion powder

Remove crusts from bread and spread generously with mayonnaise. Separate and slightly chop broccoli and press into half the slices. Sprinkle with onion powder. Top with remaining bread. Cut in quarters, or smaller sizes.

Cucumber-Mint Filling

¼ cup mayonnaise
slices of cucumber
2 tsp. minced fresh mint

Spread bread rounds with mayonnaise. Place a slice of cucumber on each round and garnish with small amount of mint.

Celery Filling

1 cup minced celery
⅛ tsp. pepper
½ tsp. salt
¼ cup mayonnaise

Combine all ingredients. Use as a spread or sandwich filling.

Carrot-Raisin Filling

2 carrots, grated
¼ cup raisins, chopped
½ cup peanut butter
mayonnaise

Combine all ingredients. Add enough mayonnaise to moisten.

English Spread

1 cup mayonnaise
1 cup grated parmesan cheese
1 clove garlic, pressed
1 can artichoke hearts, chopped

Mix together all ingredients. Warm over low heat. Serve on crackers or toast rounds.

Sweet Spreads

Apricot-Pineapple Preserve

1 lb. dried apricots
water to cover
20-oz. can crushed pineapple
½ cup sugar

Cut dried apricots in ¼ pieces. Cover with water and stew until soft, but firm. Add *undrained* crushed pineapple and sugar, continue cooking until sugar is dissolved, well blended and evaporated to a spread consistency. Store in refrigerator up to a month or freeze. Serve with muffins, scones or toast.

Yield: 3-4 cups

Pear-Kiwi Preserve

¾ cup coarsely chopped pear
1½ cups coarsely chopped kiwi
4 cups sugar
3 oz. liquid fruit pectin
½ tsp. grated lime peel
2 Tblsp. lime juice

Peel, core and chop fruits. In a large bowl, mash fruits. Stir in sugar and let stand 10 minutes. Combine the pectin, lime peel and lime juice. Add to fruit mixture and stir for 3 minutes. Ladle at once into clean hot jars, allowing a ½-inch headspace. Seal. Let stand overnight until set. Store in refrigerator up to one month. Serve with muffins, scones or toast.

Yield: 5 cups

Frosted Citrus Toast

1½ cups confectioners' sugar
1 Tblsp. butter, softened
1 tsp. grated orange peel
1 Tblsp. orange juice
1 Tblsp. lemon juice

Mix all ingredients together and store in the refrigerator. A spread for muffins, scones or toast.

HENRI HEMSCH (French, 1710–1769)
Harpsichord (double manual); linden, pine, spruce or fir, oak, pear, walnut, beech, metal, ebony, ivory, gilt, gouache, and oil paint
Gift of B. Allen Rowland

Index

Membership Application

Please print clearly

☐ Ms. ☐ Miss ☐ Mrs. ☐ Mr. ☐ Mr. & Mrs.

Name______________________________

Street______________________________

City______________________________

State____________________ Zip_______

Telephone (day)______________________

Children of age 16 and under are always admitted free.

☐ Individual $35
☐ Double $45
☐ Donor $75
☐ Reciprocal $125
☐ Supporting $250
☐ Sustaining $500
☐ Patron $1,250 and more
☐ New member ☐ Rejoining

In addition to Preview with monthly calendar, I wish to receive: ☐ Annual Report

I enclose payment of $__________ payable to the Museum of Fine Arts. Please return form and payment to: Membership Records Office, Museum of Fine Arts, 465 Huntington Avenue, Boston, MA 02115.

Order Form

**SEND A COOKBOOK TO YOUR FRIENDS
THE ORDER BLANKS BELOW ARE FOR
YOUR CONVENIENCE**

Please send ____ cookbooks @ $13.50 postpaid

to ______________________________
name

____
street address

____
city state

____
zip

from______________________________

Make checks payable and send order to

MUSEUM SHOP
MUSEUM OF FINE ARTS
465 HUNTINGTON AVENUE
BOSTON, MA 02115

Please send ____ cookbooks @ $13.50 postpaid

to ______________________________
name

____
street address

____
city state

____
zip

from______________________________